The Jane Eyre Companion

Includes Study Guide, Historical Context, and Character Index

A BookCaps™ Study Guide
www.bookcaps.com

© 2013. All Rights Reserved.

Table of Contents

Historical Context

Charlotte Brontë was the third of six children born in Yorkshire to a curate family. Her mother died and Charlotte was sent with three sisters to a school in Lancashire (which was the inspiration for Lowood School) to gain an education. However, the school's poor conditions affected their healths, and led to the deaths of her sisters Maria and Elizabeth who died of tuberculosis. After their deaths, her father removed Charlotte and Emily from the school. Back at home, Charlotte took care of her younger sisters and began creating her own fictional worlds with her siblings.

Eventually, Mary, Charlotte and Anne decided to publish a collection of poetry under pseudonyms. Charlotte's was Currer Bell, retaining her initials, but hiding her gender. While they only sold two copies of the book, they still continued to work on their first novels for publication.

Charlotte's first manuscript did not find a publisher, but they offered to read anything else that "Currer Bell" might have lying around. She sent them Jane Eyre: An Autobiography, which became a success and was well reviewed. Some reviews mentioned that the novel was shocking because it had been written in first person and was emotionally acute and accessible.

Charlotte began working on her second novel, Shirley, when three family members died. Branwell died of bronchitis and marasmus. Emily died after Branwell's funeral of pulmonary tuberculosis, and Anne died of the same disease the following week. Charlotte returned to her manuscript to try and deal with her grief. Charlotte wrote Villette afterwards which shared many similarities with Jane Eyre, including writing from the first person. Eventually Charlotte revealed her true identity because her publishers encourage her to visit London.

Charlotte married Arthur Bell Nichols, against the advice of her father, and aimed to improve her curate husband's finances by using her own connections to find him a better position. However, she grew very sick after she became pregnant and died with her unborn child at the age of 38.

Plot Overview

Short Synopsis

Jane Eyre, an orphaned child, struggles to find her place in the world. She journeys from a boarding school, to a large house with a terrifying secret, and then escapes to the country while dealing with her love for a man she should not have fallen in love with.

Detailed Synopsis

Jane Eyre was an orphan who lived with Mrs. Reed, her Aunt-in-law, at Gateshead with her three cousins, Eliza, Georgiana and John. John bullied Jane constantly for being a poor orphan who only lived with them because his mother was charitable and selfless. After Jane got into a nasty fight with John, Mrs. Reed arrived and sent Jane to the red room as a punishment. Jane begged her not to as this was the room her Uncle Reed died in. There, Jane reflected on her past and what led her to Gateshead when she thinks she sees a ghostly spirit enter the room. Jane cried out for help, terrified by the ghost, but Mrs. Reed refused to let the door be unlocked. She grew overwhelmed and faints.

Jane woke up in her own room to find that a doctor, Mr. Lloyd, had been sent for. She overheard that she is not expected to survive the night, but does so. The maid Bessie continued to treat Jane with kindness the next day, even singing her a song and giving her a tart to eat off a special plate. After Bessie leaves for dinner, Jane told Mr. Lloyd- who had returned- about the Red Room and her life as an orphan. Mr. Lloyd wondered if she wants to go to school, which Jane did. Jane had overheard the servants talking about her leaving soon.

One day, a man dressed in black named Mr. Brocklehurst arrived at Gateshead. He discussed Jane's wicked heart and bad manners. Mr. Brocklehurst admitted her into Lowood School and said would keep a close eye on her. Bessie admits that Jane was one of her favourites, even if she didn't show it, and embraces her.

Arriving at Lowood, Jane found that the school is a strict place with a lifestyle based around strict order. During class the next day, Jane watched the teacher, Miss Scatcherd, scold a student named Helen Burns off for not being clean despite having no water to wash with that morning. Burns went to a small cupboard, returned with a bundle of twigs and gave it to Miss Scatcherd who hit her with them. Burns did not cry. While Jane doesn't like that Burns doesn't fight back, they end up friends.

When Spring came you Lowood, it brought typhus with it and over half of the students ended up sick. Once the epidemic passed, it took Burns, leaving Jane with one less friend. It also resulted in an investigation that rid the school of Mr. Brocklehurst and made way for more empathetic owners who made the school a better place. Jane stayed at the school for eight years — six as a student, and two as a teacher. After her two years teaching, she decided she needed a change and got a job as a governess at a place called Thornfield manor where she teaches a girl named Adele.

Jane was impressed by the good treatment she received at Thornfield and enjoyed her work. She takes a tour of Thornfield manor one day and hears laughing and noises coming from the third story. Mrs. Fairfax- Thornfield's manager- explains that the noise is coming from one of the servants, Grace Poole. Jane often hears Poole making noises.

Mr. Rochester, the lord of Thornfield and Adele's guardian, arrives one day and the house becomes a busy place. Rochester was a blunt man whose lack of manners resulted in him criticizing Jane repeatedly when he finally took the time to get to know her. Rochester rarely stayed at Thornfield more than two weeks at a time, with him and Jane getting to know each other when he was at home. He revealed one day that Adele's mother was an old lover of Rochester from Paris whom he left after she had been unfaithful. Adele's mother claimed that Rochester was Adele's father, though he didn't believe it. When he had heard that Adele was abandoned though, he had gone to rescue her. Rochester expected Adele's illegitimacy would drive Jane away, but Jane affirmed that she would stay, knowing Adele had a hard life.

Jane saves Mr. Rochester from a fire in his bed one night, with Jane suspecting Grace Poole and Mr. Rochester agreeing. Jane then discovers she has feelings for Mr. Rochester, having grown to love him. She is surprised to see that Poole is still employed and wonders if she is blackmailing Rochester in some way. Jane learns that Mr. Rochester is staying with some friends, which includes three eligible ladies. She realizes it was silly to think that she had a chance with Mr. Rochester.

Mr. Rochester eventually returned with his friends, among them being Lady Ingram- one of the eligible ladies that Rochester could marry. Jane attempted to avoid them, but eventually she was invited to bring Adele to the drawing room one evening. Upon seeing Rochester, Jane confirms her feelings for him. Though Lady Ingram is condescending and rude, talk of Rochester marrying her is common amongst the visiting group.

Mr. Rochester left to conduct business and a man named Mr. Mason came by, saying he was from the West Indies and wanted to meet with Rochester. A gypsy woman stopped by and read the fortunes of the ladies. Lady Ingram left her private fortune reading white-faced, insisting the gypsy was a fraud. The gypsy insisted on reading Jane's fortune and said that she is keeping from reaching out and possessing a love she wants. Jane only admitted that she wanted to one day open a school. The gypsy then reveals herself to actually be Mr. Rochester. Jane mentions Mr. Mason's name, causing Mr. Rochester to be silent.

Jane receives word that her aunt- Mrs. Reed- had gone sick due to her son John committing suicide. Mr. Rochester doesn't want Jane to leave, but eventually relents. There, Jane discovers that Mrs. Reed still despises her and had in fact kept Jane from inheriting her uncle's fortune. Despite these things, Jane forgives her aunt and stays with her until she dies.

Upon returning to Thornfield, Mr. Rochester reveals that he is in love with Jane and they decide to marry. On the day of the wedding, the ceremony is stopped by Mr. Mason and a lawyer, who claim that Rochester is still married to Mr. Mason's sister, Bertha Mason. Rochester confirms that it's the truth and takes everyone to the mysterious third floor. There, Bertha Mason is cared for by Grace Poole, as Bertha has gone insane and was the one that started the fire long ago.

With nothing left, Jane left Thornfield and spent a few days sleeping outside, begging for food and wondering where she might go to find food, until she came across a house in the countryside and looked in the window. Inside was the Rivers family, consisting of Mary, Diana, and St. John. They taker her in and get her a job teaching at a charity school.

One day, St. John delivered the news that they both have a common uncle- Uncle John who had recently died. Noticing Jane's signature on one of her drawings, St. John discovered that she was the same Jane Eyre who had been willed Uncle John's fortune, making Jane wealthy. She shared her wealth with her newfound cousins. Jane moved in her with her family and they spent much happy time together. One day, St. John asked Jane to marry her, but she refused as he was in love with another woman and had no feelings for her. The disagreement caused tension, causing Jane to think of the man she truly loved.

She returned to Thornfield where she saw the burnt ruins of the manor. She learned that Bertha had caused fires all over the house. Mr. Rochester had run through the house saving everyone and went for Bertha last. There, Bertha had killed herself by jumping out the window. Pieces of the place had fallen on Mr. Rochester, causing him to lose his sight and one of his hands.

Jane went to the new home Rochester lived in and revealed herself. They affirmed their love for each other and decided to get married. Jane rescued Adele from a bad school and sent her off to a good one that treated their students well. With Jane's nursing, Rochester gained vision back in one eye, just in time to see his and Jane's new son being born.

Themes

Poverty vs. Wealth

Attitudes among and about the different classes differ throughout
Jane Eyre. Jane originally distrusts poor people as a child because
she did not know how they could be kind and later learns that they
are some of the kindest, hard-working people she has ever met. Mr.
Rochester, his friends and the Reed family are generally unkind to
Jane which suggests that their wealth is either a burden on them, or
has turned them away from kind people and feelings. When Mr.
Rochester first asks Jane to marry him, he wants to shower her with
jewels, and the second time he asks her, he doesn't care about any of
that. Not only is this growth based on the loss of his eyesight and
vanity, it is also because he has learned that none of his wealth
makes him as happy as Jane makes him.

Marriage and Love

Mr. Rochester does not love his lunatic wife, but thought he might have when he first met her. He searches for love in other places and shuts her away. St. John doesn't take love into consideration when he looks for a wife. He only looks for someone with common sense and a good work ethic. Essentially, for him, it is a contract between two people who understand their tasks and do them accordingly. Mr. Rochester falls in love with Jane and wants to marry her immediately, despite the fact that he is already married. His reasoning and sense fly out the window when it comes to making Jane is own. Jane cannot marry St. John because it would be a marriage of duty, not of love, and it is only when Jane is secure financially and has family connections that she feels she can return to Mr. Rochester without being overwhelmed and influenced without her permission. She returns to him on equal footing, and in fact, Mr. Rochester depends on her for many months until he regains some of his sight, giving Jane some of her power in the relationship back to her.

Ownership of the Body and Confinement

There are several moments where Jane, or other characters, are confined or controlled by others. St. John wants to influence Jane completely and reveals his masculine need to control his wife. Jane begins the novel trapped in the red room, and is often trapped and kept from happiness by her poor status. She cannot marry Mr. Rochester at first, for example, because she cannot compete with Blanche Ingram. When Bertha Mason is revealed to be locked up in the attic of Thornfield Hall, a pattern starts to emerge that questions the need for the female body to be controlled or coerced into certain things. As a result, Jane always tries to find a way to be matched up with an equal — she writes to her Uncle Eyre to secure her own fortune when Mr. Rochester asks her to marry him, and she can only argue with St. John once she knows he is flesh and blood and not made of stone. Jane is also confined by her social status and her gender: whereas she could have gone to India with St. John if she was a man, she cannot go as a woman unless she is related to him.

Family

Jane's quest for family informs many of her decisions in this novel. Jane has no family when she begins, but she lives with people who should have accepted her as a relative. She then goes to Lowood where the students and teachers become like a family, but her maternal figure, Miss Temple, leaves her when she marries. Jane is lost again without a structured family around her. She finds another when she arrives at Thornfield, with Adele like a daughter to her and Mrs. Fairfax like a mother, but when she falls in love with Mr. Rochester and realizes she has to leave him, this family is a threatened one for her. It's fitting, then, that she returns to Gateshead to reconcile with her Aunt before her death. Her Aunt won't admit she was cruel to Jane in the past, so she cannot show any love to Jane. Her daughters, while opening up a mild friendship with Jane, are no true sisters and flee the house after their mother's death anyway, sending Jane back to Thornfield. She then finds family in Diana, Mary and St. John, but St. John threatens this when he wants Jane for his wife. She escapes back to Mr. Rochester, the man she loves, to protect herself from him and finds a true family in him. They have their own children together and never tire of one another.

This constant need for connection and love in Jane's life stems from her childhood when she was starved of affection and family at Gateshead, and then at Lowood School, and until she finds a genuine one, she cannot rest.

Fortune

Mr. Rochester fell into a loveless marriage with a lunatic because of his family's need for a fortune for him. Blanche Ingram made a show of being in love with Mr. Rochester because he was supposed to be rich, and dropped him the minute it was suggested otherwise. These two examples of people already fortunate enough than the majority of their fellow human beings shows a kind of selfishness that ignores their own feelings for material gain. Diana, Mary and Jane, however, use their small fortunes to finance their studies and to live together. It does not separate them, but brings them closer together. Jane's selflessness when she receives her twenty thousand pounds and splits it among her cousins shows her strength of character and her fear of turning into people like her cousin, John Reed, who became so obsessed with spending money that it cost his family most of their own fortune and him his life.

Religion

Jane comes across many approaches to religion during her journey. Mr. Brocklehurst's hypocritical approach to Christianity has him spouting off religious sermons at one moment, and then denying his starved, cold students proper food and clothing to show them self sacrifice while he and his own family dress and act extravagantly. Helen Burns' approach to absolute forgiveness and submission teaches Jane that forgiveness is a good path to take, even though she doesn't agree with giving in completely, and she frequently forgives others for what they have done, including her Aunt Reed. It is no accident that Helen's path leads to her death: she lets others punish her and suffers in silence, and it eventually kills her. St. John sees religion as a place for common sense, reason and principle, and excludes any emotions that might get in his way, and Jane rejects his approach to spirituality and his hand in marriage. Jane, herself, seems to pick up on the elements of Christianity that work best for her and she constantly asks for guidance.

The Supernatural

There are many strange spiritual moments and elements in Jane
Eyre that are not explained. There is a moment between Jane and
Mr. Rochester where they hear one another's voices across the
country, and while it unnerves Jane, it's never really clear if this was
due to their shared belief in God, or for another reason. Jane never
mentions her end of the story to Mr. Rochester, and she moves on
with the story. Jane also experiences visions of certain things during
the novel, too, including a white light she believes is her Uncle Reed
in the red room, and the figure who appears to her in her room at
Thornfield to warn her against temptation. It is not known why
exactly Jane sees these things, or if they are related to Christianity,
and they may even simply be elements of the gothic novel that
Brontë wanted to employ.

Fire

While usually considered a destructive element, fire is the thing that
brings Mr. Rochester and Jane closer together. They are much more
intimate following the fire in Mr. Rochester's bedroom — to the point
where she is in his room in the dark at night — and the fire at
Thornfield brings them to a more equal footing and leads to Bertha's
death, releasing Mr. Rochester from his marriage and freeing him to
marry Jane. It is heat and passion that gives Jane the life she wants,
and the people that best exhibit these qualities end up her friends.
In contrast, colder people like St. John frighten her because they
appear inhuman until pushed to extremes.

Beauty

Blanche Ingram is a very beautiful woman, but is cruel to children and to Jane—who cannot possibly be a threat to her marriage to Mr. Rochester, but is still hated on sight. She is snooty and looks down her nose at those who she feels are stupid. Bertha Mason was a beautiful woman who had a gnarled, mad inside. Both of these women use their beauty to disguise the ugliness of their insides. Jane, on the other hand, is repeatedly referred to as plain by those around her, but her mind, intelligence and wit are attractive. While Mr. Rochester had originally married Bertha because she was beautiful and wanted by all the other men around her, he sees that Jane is a beautiful woman inside. When Mr. Rochester loses his eyesight, it symbolizes his need to see beyond the physical qualities of the people he loved, and to look inside them instead.

Substitute Mothers

Jane frequently comes across or seeks out maternal figures who might take the place of the mother she lost so young and give her guidance. Bessie scolded Jane often, but it was clear that they cared about one another. Bessie teaches Jane to find comfort in stories and songs, and their parting when she leaves for Lowood is a hard one for both of them. Miss Temple teaches Jane to be calm, focused and fair to others, and when she leaves Lowood, she feels she has to go out into the world. Mrs. Fairfax seems like she might be Jane's next maternal figure, but she loses some of her companionship with the woman when she is engaged to Mr. Rochester. Jane learns a great deal from these women in her life as she might have learned from her own mother, and her knowledge helps guide her from trouble toward the life of happiness and love she always wanted.

Character Summaries

Jane Eyre

Jane Eyre is an orphan and without any family but the Reeds, who reject her as one of them after her Uncle's death. At first, Jane is outspoken and volatile, and then too calm and measured, and finds herself by the end of the novel with a good mix of reason and passion. She is an intelligent woman who struggles to find her place in the world, and to find family and love within it, and asserts herself throughout this journey. She also strongly believes in equality among genders and social status, even if those around her do not.

Mr. Edward Rochester

Mr. Rochester suffers from extremely changing moods in part because of his tormented existence and continues to make rash decisions that impact his happiness. The knowledge that his wife of fifteen years is a mad woman and locked in his own house depresses him so he seeks happiness wherever he can find it, no matter the affect on other people around him. When he realizes there are consequences to blindly reaching for what he loves, he starts to ask for forgiveness from God and stops acting so recklessly.

St. John Rivers

St. John Rivers takes Jane in to his own home after her escape from Thornfield, provides her with a job as a schoolmistress, and even uncovers the mystery of her real identity. In doing so, he gives Jane three cousins. His coldness and love of informed reason keep him at arm's length from his own family members, but his desire to do good for the world suggests there is a passion underneath his cold exterior. He is also controlling, especially with Jane. St. John ends up in India as a missionary following his life's ambition and eventually dies.

Mrs. Reed

Mrs. Reed is Jane's Aunt-in-law and the mother to three children herself. She hates Jane because her husband loved her more than his own children, and spends most of her life trying to sabotage Jane and make her life a misery. However, when she realizes the cruelty she inflicted on the girl, she does try to mend her ways, but it's clear that this is out of fear for her soul rather than out of love for Jane.

Georgiana Reed

Georgiana is one of three Reed cousins, and the most beautiful. She tries to elope with a young lord she has fallen in love with and is stopped by her sister, Eliza. She blames Eliza for ruining her chances and only thinks about finding herself a good match in London—even when her mother lies on her deathbed and her brother just killed himself. Although Georgiana mistreated Jane when they were younger and is in need of looking at her priorities, Georgiana is a fairly sweet girl who means well.

Eliza Reed

Eliza is the other of Mrs. Reed's two daughters, and is less beautiful than her sister Georgiana. She devotes herself to the Church, spends her days studying in a strict schedule and resents her sister, who she sees as a selfish, lazy girl who has failed to apply herself to anything in her life. After their mother dies, Eliza vows never to see her sister again and goes to a convent, giving her life to the Church.

John Reed

John Reed is very cruel to Jane in their childhood and tries to beat her up at every chance he gets because he knows he'll get away with it. Jane later discovers that he left for college and began racking up debt due to drinking and gambling. When Mrs. Reed refuses to give him any more of their money, he commits suicide.

Helen Burns

Helen Burns was Jane's childhood friend at Lowood school. She teaches Jane about absolute forgiveness, and Jane is angry that she suffers her punishments in silence. When Helen contracts consumption, Jane goes to see her and is convinced Helen won't die because she is so quiet and passive. Helen dies while next to a sleeping Jane.

Bertha Mason

Bertha Mason, or Bertha Rochester, is Mr. Rochester's wife and the lunatic locked up on the third storey of Thornfield Hall. She has transformed into a wild, violent woman who lashes out at those around her and has to be protected from others and herself. She is looked after by Grace Poole, but after Grace passes out from drinking too much, Bertha escapes and sets fire to Thornfield and throws herself to her death.

Mr. Brocklehurst

Mr. Brocklehurst is the owner of Lowood school and teaches those around him and at the school the nature of self-sacrifice. In the meantime, he steals money from the school to support his family's lavish needs, and parades his well dressed wife in front of the starving, thinly dressed students. When typhus spreads through Lowood school and kills half of the students, the poor conditions at Lowood are exposed and the school is refurbished, but not by his own doing.

Mrs. Fairfax

Mrs. Fairfax is the housekeeper of Thornfield Hall. Jane originally thinks Mrs. Fairfax owns Thornfield, and is surprised but happy to find she is on a more equal footing with Jane. Mrs. Fairfax loves company and friendship, and she provides Jane with many pieces of advice that help her in her Thornfield stay. After Jane leaves, Mrs. Fairfax is sent away from the house with a salary and is never heard from again.

Adele Varens

Adele Varens is the illegitimate child of a French opera-dancer, and Mr. Rochester's ward. She is unfocused and excitable when Jane first comes to be her governess, but she calms down over time so that Jane can teach her. She is obsessed with fine things like dresses and Jane often scolds her for her vanity. When Adele is sent away to school and is mistreated, Jane rescues her and places her in a more suitable, nurturing school.

Blanche Ingram

Miss Blanche Ingram is an accomplished, beautiful woman and one of two daughters to Lady Ingram. She catches Mr. Rochester's eye and there are rumours of their impending marriage that continue for many months. When Blanche visits Mr. Rochester disguised as a gypsy woman and he hints that Mr. Rochester does not have as large a fortune as she thought, Blanche shows her true colours and breaks away from him. She looks down on those she thinks are stupid and lower class, and has no genuine feelings for those around her.

Diana and Mary Rivers

The Rivers sisters are kind, intelligent and driven women who care deeply for those around them and delight in things that make them happy. They are very different to their brother, St. John, in this way, and do not care if their excitement upsets him. They are originally governesses when Jane first meets them, but dream of independence so they can devote themselves to their studies. When Jane gives them both five thousand pounds, they return to Moor House to do exactly that.

Chapter Summaries

Chapter One

Jane- who acts as the novel's narrator- describes how she dislikes taking walks on cold days like the one taking place because of the bad weather and the fact that she'll be scolded by the nurse Bessie and made to feel inferior to her cousins.

Eliza, John and Georgiana (Jane's cousins) were gathered around their mother, Mrs. Reed, who sat on a sofa by the fire. Jane was not allowed to come closer as the privilege of being close to Mrs. Reed was reserved for only "happy children," as Mrs. Reed described it. Jane asked what Bessie said she had done, but Mrs. Reed told her to keep quiet if she was only going to question her elders.

Jane slipped into the breakfast room and took a book off the bookcase. She sat with her legs crossed on the window-seat and drew the curtains so she could hide. Jane was fairly happy to have a book like Bewick's to herself, but the moment didn't last. She was interrupted by the breakfast door opening, and John Reed calling for her. He paused, thinking the room was empty. Jane hoped that she would not be discovered, but came out from her hiding place at once so that John would not drag her out.

Jane asked him what he wanted. John wanted her to come stand before him, and to call him Master Reed. John was fourteen years old — four years older than Jane — and a schoolboy. He was large for his age with poor skin, mostly because he stuffed himself with food. He should have been at school but Mrs. Reed kept him home for a month or two on account of his poor health. John did not show much affection to his sisters or to his mother, and definitely did not like Jane; he bullied her constantly. Jane was afraid of him and did not know what she could do against him. The servants did not want to offend John by standing up to him, and Mrs. Reed never saw John attack Jane, even when he did it in her presence.

Jane walked up to John. He spent three minutes sticking his tongue out at her. Jane knew that he would hit her, but did not know when. Jane wondered if he knew what she was thinking about as he lashed out at her then. Jane staggered back, but recovered, now a step or two away from his chair. John told her he was punishing her for the way she talked back to Mrs. Reed, for hiding behind the curtains, and for the way she looked at him. Jane did not attempt to reply: she was only concerned with preparing herself for the next strike. John asked her what she was doing behind the curtain. Jane told him she was reading. John asked to see the book, so Jane fetched it. John told her she had no right to read their books as she depended on them for everything as she was an orphan. John thought she should be out on the streets, begging for money — not living in luxury, wearing clothes and eating at their expense.

John vowed to teach her for going through his bookshelves — they were his, he claimed, or would be his when the house belonged to him. He told her to stand by the door, out of the way of both the mirrors and windows. Jane did, but then realized what he was going to do: he was going to throw the book at her! She did not have enough time to move, however, and the book hit her hard enough to send her falling. She struck her head against the door, cutting it enough to draw blood. She called John a wicked murderer, compared him to slave-driver and to the Roman Emperors themselves. He runs at her and grabs her hair and shoulder. Jane felt blood trickling down her neck. She fights back but wasn't really sure what she exactly did. John cried and called her a rat. Eliza and Georgiana had gone to get Mrs. Reed, who arrived with Bessie and her maid, Abbot. Jane was blamed, and Mrs. Reed told them to lock her into the red room.

Chapter Two:

Jane struggled with Bessie and Abbot as they drag her up the entire way. Abbot told Jane off — she thought Jane should be ashamed for striking her master. Jane argued that John was not her master, and she was not his servant. Bessie and Abbot sat her on a stool in the red room, but Jane stood up again. Bessie asked her maid for her garter so they could tie her down. Suddenly terrified of being tied down, Jane assured them that she would not move, and held onto the stool with her hands to prove it.

The red room was a square room which was never slept in — unless there were enough guests at Gateshead Hall to make it necessary. It was one of the largest rooms in the house, and well decorated. Mr. Reed had been dead for nine years and had died in the red room. Since that day, the echo of the dead affected the room, and kept it from general use. Jane caught a reflection of the room in the mirror — everything looked much colder and darker in the reflection than it did in reality. Her own reflection looked like an imp or spirit from one of Bessie's stories.

Jane wondered why she was always suffering and accused of being something she wasn't. She could not please any of them. Eliza was selfish and headstrong, but she was respected. So was Georgiana, who was a spoiled, insulting child. It was her beauty that captivated others. John was never punished, even though he tortured animals, took all the fruit off their plants, tore his mother's clothing and refused to fulfill her wishes. Jane tried her best to be good, to perform her duties, and was called naughty all day. Jane wished she could run away, or let herself die.

The room was starting to get darker with the coming evening. She wondered if she was truly wicked. She had, after all, just considered starving herself to death. Jane thought about Gateshead Church. In a vault there, Mr. Reed had been buried. She could not remember him, but did remember that he was her Uncle—her mother's brother—and had taken her in when her parents had died. In his last moments, Mr. Reed begged Mrs. Reed to raise and care for Jane like one of her own children. Jane thought Mrs. Reed had done as well as her personality would allow her. Mrs. Reed saw her as an alien and an outcast in her family unit. Jane realized that Mr. Reed would have probably treated her kindly.

She looked at the bed Mr. Reed had died in and began to remember what they said about dead men who were unable to rest, especially those who had their last wishes ignored. They would often revisit the earth to punish the wicked, and Jane considered that he might appear before her in the red room. She lifted her head and looked around the dark room. A bright light gleamed on the wall. She wondered if it was the moonlight, but this light moved. It slid onto the ceiling over her head as she watched. Looking back, Jane was sure that this was a light from a lantern outside, but Jane was shaken in that moment and prepared herself for a ghost.

She panicked, rushed to the door and shook it. Bessie and Abbot entered. Bessie asked her if she was ill. Jane begged to go into the nursery, afraid that a ghost would come for her. Abbot accused her of screaming on purpose as part of a trick. Mrs. Reed arrived at that moment and told her servants the red room was meant to be locked until she came for Jane herself. She told Bessie to let Jane's hand go. Jane could not get out of the room by playing tricks on people. For her poor behaviour, Jane would be locked in the room for one more hour. Mrs. Reed pushed her back into the room and locked the door. Jane fainted.

Chapter Three:

Jane woke up feeling like she had just had a terrible nightmare. She saw a red glare with thick black bars, and heard hollow, muffled voices. Jane realized that someone was lifting her into a sitting position with more tenderness than had ever been shown to her. She realized she was in her bed. Bessie stood at the foot of the bed holding a basin. A gentleman sat in a chair near her pillow. This was Mr. Lloyd, an apothecary, who was usually called to the house when one of the servants was sick. Mr. Lloyd ordered Bessie to make sure Jane was not disturbed for the rest of the night. When he left, Jane felt very sad to lose his friendly presence. Bessie asked her if she would like to sleep. Jane told her she would try, fearful of what Bessie might say next. Bessie asked if she would like anything to drink or eat, and when Jane replied she did not need anything, Bessie assured her she could call for her anytime during the night. Jane wondered if there was something wrong with her.

When Bessie went into the servant's area, Jane overheard her say to Sarah that Jane might not survive the night. They returned to the nursery to sleep in the bed there, and were whispering to one another. Jane could only hear scraps of the conversation, but they were discussing the appearance of a spirit in the room. They fell asleep, leaving Jane to experience a long and fearful night.

Jane did not have anything wrong with her except for having a nervous disposition. By noon the following day she felt weak, but the worst of it was her sorrow. She could not stop crying even though she knew she should be happy. All of the Reeds had gone out in the carriage, Abbot was in another room and Bessie—tidying the room around her—talked to Jane every now and then with kindness. Bessie asked if she wanted a book. Bessie had finished tidying the room and began to make a new bonnet for Georgiana's doll. As she did, she sang a song. While Jane always thought her voice was sweet, it also seemed sad now. Bessie sang another song—one even sadder than the one before, and it made Jane cry by the time she finished. Bessie told her not to cry, but Jane did not know how to.

Mr. Lloyd came to visit her and asked how she was feeling. Bessie remarked that Jane seemed better, but Mr. Lloyd could see she had been crying. While Bessie thought it was because Jane could not ride in the carriage with the others, Jane assured them both that she cried because she was miserable. Once Bessie had left for dinner, Mr. Lloyd asked what made Jane fall. She told him about the haunted red room. Mr. Lloyd told her she must be a baby if she was still afraid of ghosts, and that it was silly for her to be so frightened of a dark room.

Jane admitted she was unhappy for other reasons, and Mr. Lloyd asked what those reasons were. Jane wished she could properly reply to the question, but she did not know how to. She gave him the only answer that she could: that she did not have a family. Mr. Lloyd mentioned her aunt and cousins. Jane told him that John pushed her over and her aunt locked her in the red room. Mr. Lloyd wondered if Jane thought the house was a beautiful one, and if she wasn't grateful to live in it. She argued that others had told her she did not deserve to be in it. If she had somewhere else to go, she would leave the house. Mr. Lloyd wondered if she had other relatives to go to, but Jane did not want to go and live with them if they were poor. He wondered if she would prefer them if they were kind. Jane did not know how poor people could be kind, or how she could fit in with them. Mr. Lloyd asked if she would like to go to school. Bessie had told her tales of cruelty in schools, and John Reed hated his own, but Jane had heard of ladies achieving great things. Jane agreed that she would like to attend school.

Mrs. Reed returned in the carriage and Mr. Lloyd went to speak to her. It was decided that Jane would go to school. Jane overheard Abbot talking about how Mrs. Reed had been eager to get rid of Jane — a girl she thought was always scheming and forming plots. Jane also heard that her father had been a poor clergyman, and that her mother had married him without the approval of her friends. The marriage match was considered beneath her, and her grandfather refused to give them any money. After a year of marriage, Jane's father caught typhus fever and gave it to her mother. They both died within a month of one another. Bessie thought Jane should be pitied, but Abbot would only pity her if she had been a nice, pretty child. They both agreed that, had Georgiana been in the same position, she would have raised far more sympathy.

Chapter Four:

Jane hoped that she would feel better soon — a change in her seemed near, and she waited for it to come. However, days and weeks went by and her health improved, but her state of mind did not. Mrs. Reed gave Jane a small closet to sleep in, left her to eat her meals by herself and spend time in the nursery alone while the other children were in the drawing room. Mrs. Reed did not mention school at all, but Jane felt sure that she would be sent away soon. Jane wondered what her Uncle might have to say about Mrs. Reed's treatment of Jane — she reminded Mrs. Reed that he would be watching from Heaven alongside Jane's mother and father. Mrs. Reed stared at her for a moment in fear, smacked her, and then left her alone. Bessie came into the room and told her off for an hour — to her, Jane was the wickedest child ever raised underneath a roof. Jane was tempted to believe her.

Two and a half months passed. Jane had celebrated Christmas and New Years at Gateshead, but had been excluded from most of the activities. Jane would then listen to the piano or harp being played, the servants walking back and forth across the hall and the quiet conversations going on in the drawing room. When Jane was tired of listening to all of this by herself, she left the top of the stairs and retreated to the nursery room by herself. She was sad, but not miserable.

If Bessie had been kinder, Jane would have liked to spend the evenings with her. Bessie, however, left the nursery as soon as Georgiana and Eliza had been dressed, and went down to the kitchen. She generally took the candle with her, leaving Jane with little light. She would sit with her doll on her lap until the fire died out and left the room in shadows. Jane would then undress quickly and slip into bed to escape the cold and darkness with her doll. Looking back, Jane thought it was unusual that she loved the doll so much, but guessed it was because all human beings had to love something—Jane did not have anything else to love but the doll. When Bessie was kind and gentle to Jane she thought she was one of the most wonderful people in the world. She wished that Bessie would always be the same way and would never tell her off.

Jane had not been called into Mrs. Reed's presence for three months and she wondered why she was being called now. She stood trembling in front of the breakfast room door, fearing what was behind it. She stood there for ten minutes until the constant ringing of the breakfast room bell forced her inside. When Jane stepped inside and curtseyed, she thought she saw a black pillar—it was a man, who stood straight and narrow in front of her with a grim face. Mrs. Reed explained to the stranger- named Mr. Brocklehurst- that Jane was the girl she had talked to him about. Mr. Brocklehurst interrogated Jane about her behavior, eventually deciding that she was indeed a wicked girl and would be corrected at his school- Lowood. He said Jane was accepted and then left.

Mrs. Reed and Jane were left alone in silence. Jane gathered her courage and then told Mrs. Reed she was not deceitful. If she had been, then Jane might have said that she loved her, which she did not. Jane declares she dislikes John Reed more than anyone in the world, and that Mrs. Reed was a close second. Jane goes onto challenge Georgiana's nature. Jane was grateful that Mrs. Reed was not a relative of hers. She vows never to call her "Aunt" again, and to never visit. If she is ever asked about Mrs. Reed, she shall tell them that she was very cruel.

As soon as Jane finished speaking, she felt freer than she had ever felt. Mrs. Reed looked very frightened. Her sewing had fallen on the floor, and she looked like she might cry. She asked if Jane wanted some water, and then wondered if there was anything she could do so they might be friends. Jane assured Mrs. Reed that she would let everyone at Lowood know what she has done, and what she is really like. Mrs. Reed gently suggested that Jane was passionate, which was something that must be corrected in her character, and asked if she would go and lie down. Jane did not want to lie down. She wanted to go to school and soon. Mrs. Reed agreed, under her breath, that she would go to school soon. She picked up her sewing and left the room. Jane was left alone, and victorious.

Jane stood for a moment by herself, feeling the victory. She was happy at first, but then felt sorry for having done what she did. This was the first taste of revenge for Jane, and she could have gone to Mrs. Reed to ask for forgiveness if this wouldn't increase Mrs. Reed's scorn for her. Jane decided to distract herself with a book of Arabian tales, but could not focus on the pages. She opened the glass door in the breakfast room and walked out around the trees. She could not find pleasure there, either. She did not know what to do. Bessie called out to her, then, wondering where she was. Jane did not move, and Bessie came down the path. Bessie scolded her, but Jane did not want to have to deal with Bessie's anger. She hugged Bessie and told her not to be cross. Bessie called her a strange child and asked if she was going to school. When Jane told her she was, Bessie wondered if she would be missed. Jane will not miss being scolded! Bessie explained she only scolded Jane because she was a shy, frightened child. She should be bolder.

Bessie had good news for Jane: Mrs. Reed and the children were going out to tea. Bessie has asked the cook to make a cake, and they will sit down to tea together, too. They will then pack her things as Jane had to leave Gateshead in a day or two. Bessie admits that Jane is her favorite of the children in the house, and the two happily spend the rest of the day together.

Chapter Five:

A few days later, it was barely five in the morning when Bessie came into Jane's bedroom to find her almost ready and dressed. Jane was to leave Gateshead that day at six, and Bessie was the only person who was up. Even though Bessie made her breakfast, Jane was too excited to eat. Bessie helped Jane pack some lunch and put the rest of her clothes on. They left the nursery, and as they passed Mrs. Reed's bedroom door, Bessie wondered if Jane should go in and say goodbye. Jane reveals that Mrs. Reed already visited her the previous night, told Jane to remember that they had always been best friends and to speak about her gratefully. Jane had covered her face and turned away from her. Bessie told Jane off for doing so, but Jane felt she acted correctly. Mrs. Reed had never been her friend. Jane said goodbye to Gateshead and walked through the door.

Jane did not remember much about the journey except that the day seemed unusually long. Jane fell asleep after awhile and was woken up when the coach stopped. Jane looked around her as the coach left. It was dark, windy and rainy, but she could see a wall and open door in front of her. They went through this door, beyond which many buildings spread as far as the eye could see. They went into one and the servant left Jane in a room with a fire burning. Miss Miller then came in and introduced herself, asking Jane about her life and abilities.

Jane then followed Miss Miller through many halls until they reached a long room. Tables with candles burning on them stood at either end, and seated around these were groups of girls. There were around eighty girls and Jane was a little overwhelmed by the sight. They were all dressed in uniform and studying. Miss Miller told Jane to sit on a bench by the door, and then called to the monitors to collect lesson books and hand out the supper trays. They all drank from the same mug, and shared fragments of oak cake amongst them. Jane went into the bedroom but was too tired to really look around her. She knew that the room was long, however, and that there were many rows of beds. Jane would sleep in the same bed as Miss Miller that night.

The next time she woke up, it was not even dawn. Bells rang, and the girls were up and dressing themselves. Jane got up and dressed, even though it was very cold. Another bell rang and the girls lined up in twos, walked down the stairs and entered the schoolroom. Each student held a book, and a book like a Bible sat on each table in front of them before an empty seat. After a moment, a bell rang and three ladies entered the room and went to the empty seat. Miss Miller told Jane to join this class. They had passages from the book read, and then read chapters in the Bible for about an hour. After this had been done, the day had finally started properly. The bell rang again, and the groups were marched to another room for breakfast. Jane was glad, because she was starving and had not eaten much the day before.

They were led into a room with two long tables where bowls of hot food sat on the table, but it smelt disgusting. The taller girls whispered to each other that the porridge was burnt again, but one of the teachers called for silence. The other teachers joined the tables, a prayer was said and then the meal began. Burnt porridge to Jane was as bad as rotten potatoes. Each girl tried to swallow her own food, but most of them gave up trying to eat their breakfast. As Jane left the room with the others, she saw one of the teachers taste the porridge and declare it was disgusting.

When they returned to the classroom, the children had fifteen minutes to talk amongst themselves, and the breakfast was complained about loudly. When the clock struck nine, Miss Miller called for silence. In five minutes, everything was back in order. The girls sat very still and quietly. Jane wondered why nothing was happening, and took the time to look around at them. They all wore the same uniform, which suited the younger girls, but made the other girls look odd. Suddenly, everyone stood at the same time, even though no one had ordered them too. The classes then sat again, and Jane was aware that they were all looking in the same direction: at the lady Jane came across the previous night. Miss Miller returned to her place, and called for the globes to be brought out. While this was happening, the lady moved slowly across the room. Jane admired her: she was tall, pretty, wore a fashionable dress and had a watch hanging from her girdle. This was Miss Maria Temple, as Jane would later learn. She was the superintendent of Lowood School. She took a seat in front of a table and started to give a geography lesson to the first class. Other teachers taught the classes history, grammar, writing, and maths, until the clock struck twelve.

The school garden was a wide area and surrounded by walls on every side. Jane looked up at the school building: a new section had been built onto the old building. She read the tablet above the door: it called for light, or goodness, to shine before men so that they can see the good work you have done. Jane read it over and over. Jane turned to find a girl sitting near her on a stone bench, bent over a book. Jane could see that the title of it was "Rasselas". She asked the girl if the book was interesting, and what it was about. It was odd for Jane to talk to a stranger, but they both shared a love of reading — even if Jane was not interested in reading anything serious. The girl handed Jane the book to look at. Jane did, but found nothing of interest to her: there were no fairies or genies, and nothing colourful. Jane handed it back to her and asked the girl what the inscription above the door meant, and what Lowood Institution referred to. The girl explained that it was the name of the school. Jane asked her many other questions and discovered that the school was a charity school, the pupils were orphans and sponsored by either upper class people in the area, or paid their own way. The bell rang and they went back inside.

The dinner was no more appetizing than the breakfast had been. Two large vessels sat on the tables with potatoes and shreds of rusty meat in them. Jane ate what she could and wondered if every day would be the same. They continued classes until five. During these classes, the girl with the book had been sent away from Miss Scatcherd's history class and made to stand in the middle of the room. Jane thought that the girl — who looked thirteen or older — would be distressed by this punishment, but she remained quiet and still. Jane knew if she was in that position, she would have wanted the ground to swallow her up. Jane wondered if the girl was daydreaming. After five, they had some coffee and a bit of bread, but Jane was still hungry when she went to bed.

Chapter Six:

The next day was the same as the one that came before, but without washing as the water in the pitchers had frozen over. At first the classes seemed too long and difficult for her, and Jane was glad when Miss Smith placed a border of muslin and thread into her hands and asked her to hem it quietly. All but one class sat and did the same. This class sat around Miss Scatcherd and read. The girl Jane had met yesterday was sat at the top of the class, but after she read aloud incorrectly, she was sent to the bottom. Miss Scatcherd continued to pick on her, though, constantly criticizing her. Jane discovered that the girl's last name was Burns.

After the chapter had been read twice, the books were closed up and the girls were tested. Burns answered all the questions well, and Jane thought Miss Scatcherd would compliment her on it. Instead, she called Burns dirty for not cleaning her nails that morning. Miss Scatcherd then started providing orders. Burns immediately left the class, went to a small room were books were kept and carried a bundle of twigs back into the room. She gave them to Miss Scatcherd with a curtsey, and then, without being told to, removed her pinafore. The teacher hit her across the neck with the twigs a dozen times or more. Burns did not cry, but when she carried the twigs back, Jane could see a single tear on her cheek.

That evening, while groups of students gathered together to talk, Jane wandered between them without a friend of her own. She did not feel lonely, however, and looked out the windows now and then. Jane knelt beside one of the fires and found Burns absorbed in a book, away from everyone else. Jane asked her if she was still reading "Rasselas", and Burns replied she was, but had just finished it. Jane thought that she might be able to get the girl to talk some more now, and asked her more questions.

The girl's name was Helen Burns, and she had come from a place close to Scotland. Jane wondered if she wanted to leave Lowood but Helen did not know why she would as Lowood was a place to gain her education. Jane declared she would have taken the rod and broken it in two if she had been in the same position as Helen had earlier. Helen did not think she would, but if she did, Mr. Brocklehurst would expel her from the school. Helen explains it is better to endure pain that only you can feel, rather than to take action which might affect others. Helen argues that it is weak to say she cannot bear something which she will be required to bear in the future. Jane could not understand or sympathize with Helen. Helen tells her that she never puts things back in order, is careless, forgets the rules, and reads too much. These provoke Miss Scatcherd who is neat, punctual and particular. After speaking to Jane about Miss Temple and why she doesn't fight back, Helen's head dropped then, and Jane thought she wanted to be left alone with her thoughts. She wasn't allowed much time to think, however, as a large, rougher girl came up and threatened to tell Miss Scatcherd if she did not put her things in order. Helen sighed, but got up and went to tidy her things.

Chapter Seven:

Jane's first few months at Lowood were spent struggling with new rules and tasks. Jane's fear of failure was greater than her physical hardship. The snow during the first few months prevented Jane from going outside except for church services. When they went to church, their clothes and shoes were not sufficient enough to keep the cold and snow out, and they were numb by the end of it. They had scarcely any food to eat, and whenever the hungry bigger girls threatened the younger ones, they took their portions of food too. In these moments, Jane shared out her portion to those who had none, and cried in secret when the hunger became too much.

Sundays were spent walking two miles to Brocklehurst Church. On their return walk to Lowood, Miss Temple would walk up and down the line trying to cheer the others up. The other teachers were generally unable to cheer others. When they finally arrived, the bigger girls huddled together around the fire, blocking access to the younger girls. The evening was spent repeating passages by heart and listening to a long sermon by Miss Miller. Many of the girls — overpowered by the need to sleep — fell to the floor. They were propped up by the monitors after being forced into the centre of the schoolroom.

Jane was relieved that Mr. Brocklehurst had not visited, but one afternoon he finally did. He stepped into the room while Jane was working out a sum. He whispered into Miss Temple's ear, and Jane was afraid that he was speaking about her, especially considering his earlier conversation with Mrs. Reed. However, as Jane was quite close to them, she overheard most of what was said. Mr. Brocklehurst asked her not to hand the girls too many needles, or they might lose them, and to be more careful with their clothes. He went on to ask her not to give the children more than one pair of clean clothes in a week. He asked Miss Temple about the lunches of bread and cheese. Miss Temple admitted that this was her doing as the breakfast was inedible. Mr. Brocklehurst explained that his plan was to bring up the girls without luxury and to make them hardy, patient and self-denying. By providing something to eat after a disappointing spoiled meal, they do not learn. Mr. Brocklehurst would prefer her or one of the other teachers to remind the girls about the suffering of Christians in the past.

Mr. Brocklehurst stared out at the school, too, and suddenly saw something that shocked him. He pointed to a girl, hand shaking, and asked why she had curly hair. It was a defiance to him when all the other girls had their hair as they should — close, tidy and modest. Miss Temple pointed out that the girl's hair was naturally curly, but Mr. Brocklehurst would not have it. He decided he would send a barber along to cut her hair. He then told her to order the first class to stand and face away from him so he could see all of their hair. He ordered other girls to have their hair cut. Miss Temple seemed to disagree, so he argued that he had to teach these girls not to be vain or waste time on their hair.

Three ladies stepped in, then, and were dressed finely. They were led to seats of honour at the top of the room, and began to tell Miss Smith that she needed to take better care of the linen and the dormitories. While this was going on, Jane held the slate in front of her face to hide, but the slate fell from her hand and snapped into two. Mr. Brocklehurst called her careless, and reminded himself that he had something to say about her. He called Jane forward. Two of the bigger girls pushed her towards him, and Miss Temple helped her along. She told Jane not to be afraid as it was a simple accident. Mr. Brocklehurst asked for a stool to be brought to him, and made Jane stand on it. Mr. Brocklehurst asked the school to look at Jane. He warned them against Jane, who he said was not a member of God's flock, but an alien. Students must avoid her company and exclude her from everything. Teachers must watch her and scrutinize all of her actions, and punish her body to save her soul. Jane, he told them, was a liar.

There was a ten minute pause, then, where most in the room whispered and looked at her. Mr. Brocklehurst continued. He told them that Mrs. Reed had raised the child out of charity like her own daughter, and Jane had been ungrateful for it. Mrs. Reed had separated Jane from her own children out of fear that their purity would be destroyed. After this, he stood and, followed by his family, walked out of the room. Before he left, he told her to stand for half an hour longer on the stool.

When the girls walked past her, Jane felt like a slave or victim under the scrutiny of martyrs and heroes. Jane lifted her head and stood firmly on the stool. Helen Burns smiled at her as she walked past: it was a smile of intellect and courage. Helen wore the untidy badge on her arm—Miss Scatcherd had condemned her to a dinner of bread and water the next day because she had messed up copying an exercise out. Jane thought that man was born imperfect, and only someone like Miss Scatcherd could see the minute defects and ignore the good.

Chapter Eight:

After school was dismissed, Jane went into a corner and sat down on the floor while the rest of the school had tea in the refectory. The courage that had kept Jane on the stool suddenly left her, and she started to cry. Jane had meant to be good, to do everything she could at Lowood and make friends. She had even made progress that morning by advancing to the head of the class. Miss Miller and Miss Temple had both praised her and promised to teach her drawing and French. Jane did not think she would ever manage to rise from the floor again.

Helen Burns came to her and gave her some coffee and bread to eat. Jane could not, fearing she might choke. Helen sat on the floor next to her. Jane asked why she stayed with a girl everyone thought was a liar. Helen pointed out that there were millions who had not heard what Mr. Brocklehurst had to say. Jane did not care about the millions—only the eighty she had to deal with. Helen insisted that they probably pitied her more than anything. Mr. Brocklehurst was not a good man, and was not liked. If he had treated her nicely, Jane would have made enemies. Teachers and students might look at her with coldness for a few days, but most would come around in the end. They held hands. Helen assured Jane that even if the world did think she was a liar, she would still have friends. Jane would rather die than live without love: she would have her arm broken if it meant she would have the love of others. Helen told her not to think too much about the love of other human beings and to stop being impulsive. Even if others mistreated her, angels would see the innocence in her heart. God only waits for their bodies and souls to be separated so that he can reward them. Helen had calmed Jane down, but she sounded very sad. She coughed, and Jane was immediately worried for her. They held one another and sat in silence. They had not been sitting there for long when Miss Temple stepped in and ordered them back to their rooms.

They followed her to her apartment. There was a good fire going, and they gathered around it. Miss Temple wondered if Jane had cried her grief away, but Jane did not think she could ever do that as everyone thought she was wicked. Miss Temple assured her they would think of her how seems and proves herself to be. They discussed Mrs. Reed, and Miss Temple asks Jane to tell her the truth of what happened. When Jane mentioned Mr. Lloyd, who came to visit Jane when she was sick, Miss Temple suggested she knew him. She decides to write a letter to him to see if he agrees with Jane's statement. If he does, Jane will be publicly cleared. Miss Temple required no further evidence, however, and assured Jane she believed in her.

Miss Temple then asked Helen if she had coughed much that day, and if the pain in her chest was better. Helen said she felt better, but Miss Temple still stood up and examined her. She was not pleased by what she found, but did not say anything. She rang a bell and asked for toast and tea, but they did not bring enough for three, nor would they provide more. Miss Temple was well prepared, however, and removed a seed cake from a drawer and cut them generous sizes. When tea was over, they settled in front of the fire and Jane listened as Miss Temple and Helen spoke. She was amazed by both of them, but particularly with Helen. Her cheeks were bright, when they had only been pale before. They talked about nations, histories, and books. Jane's amazement reached its peak when Miss Temple wondered if she remembered her Latin, and asked her to read from Virgil. When the bell rang for bedtime, she hugged them both and blessed them. She held Helen a little longer than Jane and seemed very sad.

When they reached the dormitory, Miss Scatcherd was going through their drawers. She reached through Helen Burns', criticized her, and told her that she would have six untidy articles pinned to her shoulder the next day. The next morning, Miss Scatcherd wrote the word "Slattern" on a board and bound it around Helen's forehead. She wore it until the evening and thought it was a deserving punishment. The moment Miss Scatcherd left the room, she walked over to Helen and tore it off. Jane threw it into the fire, and cried because Helen's humiliation hurt Jane so much.

About a week after Miss Temple wrote to Mr. Lloyd, he replied. The reply appeared to defend Jane's statement, so Miss Temple assembled the entire school and announced that Jane was cleared of every charge against her. The teachers shook hands with her, and the students seemed very happy. After this, Jane grew determined to work hard through everything. Her memory and wits improved and in a few weeks she advanced to a new class. She began to study French and drawing. Instead of imagining a sumptuous feast to curb her hunger, Jane began to imagine drawings in her head. Jane would never wish to exchange Lowood for Gateshead again.

Chapter Nine:

The hardships at Lowood decreased. Spring was steadily approaching and had melted the snow already. Jane's feet began to heal, and the nights and mornings were not so cold. Every morning there was new growth in the gardens outside. On Thursday afternoons, they took walks and Jane took delight in the countryside beyond the garden walls. April gave way for a warm May, and everywhere she looked, Jane saw flowers and greenery around Lowood's grounds. Unfortunately for Lowood's students, the fog brought on sickness and typhus. As the students had been fairly starved and had been neglected, just over half of the girls were sick. Classes and rules were relaxed at this time. Those who were able to leave and stay with friends and relatives did so, but the ones who remained and were well were encouraged to exercise more frequently. Miss Temple took care of the sick. Some students died and were buried quietly and quickly. Jane and the others who were well rambled through the woods like gypsies from morning until night.

Mr Brocklehurst and his family never visited Lowood, the housekeeper had fled, and her replacement was fairly liberal. There was more food to go around, and the girls would often go into the woods to eat. Jane's chosen spot was usually in the middle of the stream. She and another girl, Mary Ann, would sit on a broad stone. She liked Mary Ann because she was witty and original, and set her at ease. She was a few years older and knew more about the world than she did. She forgave Jane's flaws, and they got on well with another when telling stories and asking questions. Se had not forgotten Helen Burns, and would have spent this time with her, but Helen was ill and had been taken away to a room upstairs. She did not know which room. She could not be with the others as she was sick with consumption, and not typhus. Jane was sure she would be well again soon, especially as she came downstairs on warm, sunny afternoons and spent time with Miss Temple in the garden, wrapped up in blankets. On these times, she was not allowed to go and speak to her.

One evening, Mary Ann and Jane had been walking in the woods and had separated from the rest of the group and lost their way. When they finally made their way back to Lowood, it was quite dark. The surgeon's pony stood at the garden door. Mary Ann suggested that there must be someone very ill inside. She went into the house while Jane planted the roots she had found in the forest. She thought it was sad for someone to be dying while the world was so pleasant. Jane heard the front door open. Mr. Bates and a nurse came out. Just as the nurse was about to close the door, Jane ran up to her and asked how Helen was. She replied that Helen was not well and would not be there much longer. Jane knew immediately that Helen was dying, and asked to see her. She was in Miss Temple's room, but the Nurse refused to let her go and speak to her.

Jane could not sleep. She got up when the others were asleep, and crept out of the room in search of Miss Temple. Her room was on the other side of the house, but Jane knew her way. She was worried about being discovered, but she had to see Helen to say goodbye. When Jane approached Miss Temple's room, she saw that the door was ajar. She pulled it open and looked in, afraid to find death there. Close to Miss Temple's bed, a small crib had been set up for Helen. Miss Temple was nowhere to be seen—Jane discovered later that she had been called away to help with a patient in the make-shift hospital. She approached the crib, went to pull the curtain back, and then thought better about it. She did not want to look at a corpse. Jane asked if she was awake. Helen pulled the curtain back. She was pale and cold, but had not changed that much. She did not think that Helen would die after all. Jane sat next to her and kissed her. She was cold and thin, but still smiled. Helen knew she had come to say goodbye before she went home—to her last home. Jane told her not to speak the way she was. Helen asked Jane to get into the bed because her feet were bare. Helen whispered to her that Jane should not grieve when she dies. They will all die one day, and at least her illness was gentle. There will be no one else to miss her as her father had just married, and at least this way she would escape suffering in her life. Helen has faith that she is headed to God, and that Jane would join her one day. Helen felt comfortable and sleepy, but did not want Jane to leave her. They kissed one another and went to sleep.

When she woke up it was day and she found herself in someone's arms. It was a Nurse. She carried Jane through the passages back to the dormitory. No one told her off for leaving her bed. One or two days afterwards, Jane learned that Miss Temple had found them both huddled together in the crib. Jane was asleep, and Helen was dead. Her grave was dug in Brocklebridge and remained unmarked until fifteen years after her death.

Chapter Ten:

Jane- as narrator- tells the reader that this will not be a full autobiography. She will pass eight years very quickly with only a few lines to explain what had happened during them.

When the typhus finally disappeared from Lowood, the number of victims drew public interest. The unhealthy nature of the school, the quality of the food, the fetid water, the student's poor clothing and living conditions were discovered, and these were beneficial to the institution. Several wealthy people in the country looked for a larger building in a better location, improvements were made in diet and clothing, the funds of school were entrusted to a committee and Mr. Brocklehurst retained his position, but had a sympathetic gentleman as a partner. The school became a useful and noble one.

Jane stayed at the school for eight years: six years as a student, and two as a teacher during which delighted in pleasing her teachers and excelling in her studies. She rose to the be the first girl in the first class, and then was given the opportunity to be a teacher. Miss Temple was a great friend and a motherly figure, but eventually married and move to a distant county. From this day, Jane was no longer the same. She was no longer settled and Lowood ceased to feel like a home to her. Jane feared that she had been borrowing Miss Temple's focus and calm and was now starting to feel like herself again now that she was gone. Jane's world at Lowood had consisted of rules and systems, but she remembered now that the world was varied and awaited those who had courage to go out into it. She opened her window and looked out. She focused on the peaks in the distance, and longed to travel the roads that disappeared into the horizon. Jane had never left Lowood since the days she arrived. She had had no other form of communication with the outside world, either. She had liked routine, but now grew tired of it. She prayed for change. To serve elsewhere. She wondered how she would accomplish it. After thinking intensely and coming to no conclusions, Jane lay down in bed. The solution struck her: she had to advertise in the paper. Satisfied, Jane finally fell asleep.

The next day she wrote her letter, went into Lowton and posted it. The next week she visited the post office to see if any letters waited for her. There was one. The letter had an F in the middle of the seal. She broke it and read. The letter reported that there was a girl under ten years of age in need of a teacher at Thornfield, near Millcote. The letter had been sent from a Mrs. Fairfax. Jane examined the document and found that the writing was old fashioned, and therefore written by the hand of an elderly lady. Jane wanted to step carefully into a new position, and working for an older lady would be a good step. Jane imagined that she was very respectable. Thornfield was probably the name of her house. Millcote was seventy miles nearer to London than where she was now, which was exactly what Jane wanted: more life, and more movement. Jane guessed that the house would be quite far from Millcote itself.

The next day, Jane told the superintendent that she had an opportunity for a job that paid double what she was paid at Lowood, and asked her to tell Mr. Brocklehurst about it. Mr. Brocklehurst told Jane that Mrs. Reed had to be asked about it as she was still her natural guardian. Mrs. Reed replied to a letter to tell him that Jane could do whatever she wanted. Formal approval was given to Jane so that she might leave, and they put together a reference for her signed by the institution's committee for Mrs. Fairfax to read over. Jane received a reply from Mrs. Fairfax telling Jane that she had the position and could start in two weeks. On the day before, Jane packed the same trunk she had brought with her eight years previous from Gateshead, prepared her travelling clothes, and tried to rest. Jane could not, even though she was tired — she was much too excited about her life's next phase.

Jane was wandering around in the school's lobby when a servant told her a person wanted to speak to her. She stepped downstairs and saw a well dressed servant. The servant took her hand, and wondered why Jane did not remember her. In another second, Jane recognized her: it was Bessie! They both went into the parlour. By the fire stood a little boy. This was Bessie's son; she was married, had a little girl as well whom she called Jane, and lived in the old lodge. Jane asked about the Reed children. Georgiana was handsome, went to London and a young lord fell in love with her. Even though family disproved of the match, Georgiana tried to run away with him. Her sister found out and stopped her. John went to college, but did not do too much with his time there and spent too much money. Jane wondered if Miss Reed had sent her, but Bessie had come before Jane went away to another part of the country. Bessie told Jane that she looked like a lady, but was not very pretty — Bessie had not expected her to be as she was not a pretty child. Although Jane did not mind the honest statement, she still wanted to please others. Bessie said she was most likely clever and could play the piano. Jane played for her, and Bessie did not think that the Reed girls could have played as well. Bessie and Jane discussed her ability to paint and speak French.

Bessie told Jane that the Eyres had made contact with the family. Even though Mrs. Reed had always said the Eyres were poor, Bessie believes they are quite rich now. Seven years ago, Mr. Eyre — her father's brother — came to Gateshead to see Jane. He was disappointed to hear that Jane was at school as he could not stay. He had to travel to a foreign country — to Madeira. Mrs. Reed called him a sneaking tradesman, but Bessie and Jane agreed he was probably a wine-merchant or a clerk to one. They talked for a moment longer. Jane saw her again the next morning at Lowton while they were waiting for the coach, and then they each went their separate ways.

Chapter Eleven:

Jane sat in a room at the George Inn in Millcote. She thought that there would be someone to meet her when she got off the coach, but there was no one at all to take her to Thornfield. She asked the waiter if there was a message for Jane, but there was nothing at all for her. The only thing she could do was to ask to be taken to a private room to wait. Jane thought it was quite strange for her to feel so unconnected from everything – the promise of adventure usually made these moments bearable, but her fear overcame her. After half an hour, she asked the waiter if he knew of somewhere called Thornfield. He disappeared to the bar to ask, and returned immediately to ask if her name was Miss Eyre. There was a person waiting for her. Jane got up quickly and walked into the inn passage. A man was standing by the open door. He lifted her luggage into the vehicle, which was a little like a car, and then they both got in.

It was an hour and a half to Thornfield, which gave Jane time to reflect. She guessed that Mrs. Fairfax was not an extravagant person, and Jane was pleased for it. She had lived with fine people before and was very miserable with them. She also wondered if Mrs. Fairfax lived alone with the little girl. Jane looked out the window, then, and saw that Millcote was far behind them. The environment was less populated and pretty than the Lowood area. They went on. Eventually the driver announced that they were close to Thornfield. Jane looked out the window and saw a Church. Ten minutes later, they passed through a set of gates and came to a long house.

A servant opened the door, and then led her into the house, across a hall and into a room lit by a fire and several candles. A small old lady — exactly the way Jane had imagined her — sat in a chair knitting. She got up to greet Jane and asked her to sit by the fire. She removed Jane's bonnet and shawl herself, even though Jane told her she didn't need to. Jane had not expected to be welcomed as well as she was, and was pleased for it. She had not heard of any governesses being treated in this way, but Mrs. Fairfax didn't seem to think anything of it. Jane asked if she would see Miss Fairfax, her student, that night, but Mrs. Fairfax revealed that her student's name was actually Miss Varens. Mrs. Fairfax had no family of her own. Jane thought that she could have asked how she was related to Miss Varens at this moment, but then remembered it was impolite to ask too many questions.

Mrs. Fairfax commented that it would be nice to have someone else to talk to at Thornfield. There were servants, but Mrs. Fairfax did not want to talk to them too much for fear of losing her authority over them. When the child came to Thornfield it had made things better, but Jane would improve matters considerably. Mrs. Fairfax had arranged for the room next to hers to be Jane's. It was better than the larger rooms, which were usually dreary. She led Jane out of the room and through the house to her bedroom. The house was quite cold and reminded Jane of a Church. She was pleased to find her room was small and looked more modern. Mrs. Fairfax wished her a good night and left Jane to herself. Finally she felt safe, and knelt on the floor to pray and gave thanks for her safe journey.

The next day, Jane dressed herself well enough to look neat and tidy. She regretted that she did not look prettier, and that she was so tiny, pale and odd looking. She did not know why she wanted to look prettier; when she thought she looked well enough for Mrs. Fairfax and her new pupil, she left her room. She looked around the house at the pictures and decorations. Jane thought everything looked elegant. The house was three storeys high with stately grounds. Hills surrounded Thornfield a little like Lowood and gave it a lonely sort of atmosphere. Jane had not expected that, but she still enjoyed the calming environment. On top of one of the hills sat an old church. Jane was enjoying the view when she noticed Mrs. Fairfax at the door.

After a brief conversation about Thornfield, Mrs. Fairfax commented that she was afraid that the house would end up needing repairs soon if Mr. Rochester didn't start living there more permanently. Jane asked who Mr. Rochester was. Mrs. Fairfax revealed he was the real owner of Thornfield. Jane was surprised — she had thought Mrs. Fairfax owned Thornfield. Mrs. Fairfax revealed she was the housekeeper. She was distantly related to the Rochesters on his mother's side, but that was it. The pupil, Miss Varens, was Mr. Rochester's ward, and he had asked for a governess to be hired for her. Jane was pleased that Mrs. Fairfax was just like her — a servant — because they could communicate on an equal footing. At this moment, Jane's pupil and her nurse came running up the garden toward them.

She was about seven or eight years old, with a small build and lots of hair. The little girl, Adele, spoke in French. Jane was amazed they were foreigners. Mrs. Fairfax explained that Adele had not left Europe until six months previous. She did not even speak English before she came to England. When Adele discovered that Jane was her governess, she shook Jane's hand. She led Adele into breakfast and asked some questions in French. After ten minutes or so, Adele suddenly lit up and exclaimed that Jane knew French as well as Mr. Rochester did. It was also a god send to Sophie, too, as no one else understood her. Adele talked almost without taking a breath about her journey to England. Mrs. Fairfax was amazed that Jane could follow the conversation. Adele used to live with her mother, but she died. She used to teach Adele how to sing and dance, and both of them used to sing for gentlemen and ladies. She asked Jane if she wanted to hear Adele sing. Jane did. Adele sat on Jane's knee, shook her curls back and began to sing opera. The song was about a lady who wants to wear jewels and clothing to show a man who cheated on her that she did not care about him. Jane thought the subject was odd for a child. When she finished, Adele recited some poetry, which showed she had been well trained. Her mother taught her how to recite. Jane stopped her from dancing afterwards and asked her more questions. She discovered that Adele had lived with another couple after her mother's death until Mr. Rochester asked her to live with him in England. She knew him before her mother's death, and he used to give her presents of dresses and toys. Adele did not think she had kept his word, though, as Mr. Rochester disappeared again after bringing her to England. She never sees him.

After breakfast, Jane and Adele went to the library, which would be used as Adele's schoolroom. One bookcase had been left unlocked and contained books Mr. Rochester had thought would be of interest to the governess and pupil. There was also a piano, a painting easel and a pair of globes. Adele was not used to discipline in her studies, so after a morning, Jane let her return to her nurse. As Jane went upstairs to fetch her things to draw, Mrs. Fairfax called out to her. Jane went into the room she was cleaning. It was the dining room. Mrs. Fairfax explained that neither this room or some of the others were ever used. It was a very pretty room, and well taken care of. Mrs. Fairfax liked to keep the rooms in order as Mr. Rochester sometimes arrived without notice and needed to use the rooms. He was generally well liked, the family were respected, but he was a little peculiar. Mrs. Fairfax never knew if Mr. Rochester was serious or making fun of her when they spoke, so she never really understood him. Irregardless, he was a good person to work for. Jane observed that there were some people who were unable to provide an accurate description of others, and Mrs. Fairfax fell into this group of people. Jane wondered when she would meet him for herself.

After their conversation, Mrs. Fairfax took Jane on a tour of the house. Jane thought that the house was well designed and decorated. The third storey of Thornfield Hall looked the most like a shrine to memory and the past, and Jane liked the gloom, but would never sleep in one of the rooms on that floor. Mrs. Fairfax commented that if they had ghosts at Thornfield, these were the rooms they would inhabit. She then took her above to the battlements so that Jane might see the view of the grounds more clearly then went back down the stairs. While Mrs. Fairfax locked the door to the battlements, Jane heard a laugh — first quiet, and then louder, but still low. Jane could not figure out where the noise was coming from. She asked Mrs. Fairfax what the noise was. She explained that Grace Poole, one of the servants, was often found laughing. Grace did not answer Mrs. Fairfax's call, nor did Jane expect her to, but Grace did come out of a door nearby to be chastised by Mrs. Fairfax. The moment of gloom had passed and the conversation turned to Adele, who rushed to meet them in the hall.

Chapter Twelve:

Mrs. Fairfax and Adele continued to be as they seemed. Mrs. Fairfax was kind and competent, and Adele was a spoiled child but became obedient over time. She had nothing especially particular about her to make her stand out from any other child her age, but she had no real vices to sink herself in Jane's eyes. She wanted to please Jane, and this desire gave fuel to her education. Jane cared about her welfare a great deal. However, Jane was still restless. She would often go up onto the battlements to look out beyond Thornfield's grounds and imagine towns and villages beyond the hills. She wished she had the ability to see a great deal further. Although Jane admired and was thankful for Adele and Mrs. Fairfax, she believed harder in the existence of better examples of goodness in the world. Jane knew that many would call her restless and discontented with her life, but it was in her nature to feel restless. Her only relief was to walk back and forth along the third storey corridor and allow her imagination to go wild. Jane did not think it was in human nature to be satisfied by calm..

Jane frequently heard Grace Poole's laugh, and sometimes even heard her murmuring in a strange way. Some days Jane heard nothing, but other times the noises she made Jane could not explain correctly. She would see Grace leave her room with a basin or plate, go down to the kitchen and return with a beer. Jane often tried to pull her into a conversation, but she did not speak much. When she did reply, she replied with only a few words that did not lead to further comments.

One afternoon in January, Mrs. Fairfax and Adele begged Jane for a holiday because she was sick. Jane remembered how precious her own few holidays had been as a child and agreed that Adele could have one. Jane was tired of sitting around in the house, so offered to post a letter Mrs. Fairfax had just written. She would carry it to Hay, which was two miles away. Jane walked quickly to make herself warm, and then slowed down to enjoy the walk. While the road she walked was known for its beautiful roses and blackberries, Jane thought it was a perfect wintery scene. Even if the wind blew, there were no signs of it in this leafless lane. Jane stopped half way up a hill to rest on a stile. She could see Thornfield from where she sat. She waited until the sun went down behind the trees, and then moved on.

The night was so calm that she could hear faint murmurs of people in Hay, even though it was a mile away still. She could also hear small brooks. Just as Jane left the stile, she heard a horse coming her way. She stood aside to let it pass. Memories of stories came to mind, including one of Bessie's tales about the Gytrash, a spirit which came in the shape of a horse and chased travellers. But when the horse appeared with a rider, the spell was broken. No one rode the Gytrash. He and his dog passed Jane, who turned back to Hay until she heard a sliding sound and a shout. Both the rider and his horse had slid on a sheet of ice. The dog barked, the sound echoing in the hills. Jane went to help. The rider was making an effort to free himself from under the horse, and so Jane did not think he could be that hurt, but he did not reply. Jane wanted to help him, but the man only told her to stand aside. He got to his feet, the horse got to its feet and the dog was calmed. The rider, however, appeared injured, as he went to the stile to sit. Jane offered to fetch someone from Thornfield or Hay, but the rider insisted he had only sprained his foot.

Jane observed him for a moment: he had a dark, stern face of someone past youth but not quite middle aged. Jane was not afraid of him – if he had been handsomer, and more heroic, she might not have had the courage to offer her help. She had never come across an elegant, beautiful young man, and if she had, she knew that he would never have any sympathy for her, nor should he have. Jane would have shunned them and moved on. The roughness of the traveller put her at ease. She repeated her intent to help him, but he only commented that she ought to be at her home. He asked Jane where she came from, and she replied that she came from Thornfield. He asked who owned the house. She told him that Mr. Rochester owned the house, but he did not live there, nor did she know where he was. He looked her over and concluded that she was not a servant. Jane told him she was the governess. He stood, but was still in pain. He asked her to help him along a bit: she had to take the horse's bridle and lead him to the rider, but the horse would not let her near enough. The rider laughed and asked her to help him to the horse. He placed a hand on her shoulder and leaned on her. He took the horse's bridle, asked her to find the whip, and told her to hurry to Hay to deliver her letter. The rider and the dog turned and went away.

While the moment had not been romantic, it was still a break in her monotonous life. She had been asked for help, and had willingly given it, and Jane was happy to have done something for someone else—for someone new. She went to Hay to deliver the letter, and still thought about the rider's face. Jane did not like going back to Thornfield, because it meant going back to her restless, boring life. She hesitated for a moment outside, until she had to go into the house. There was a fire lit in the dining room and a group was gathered near the mantelpiece. She did not have enough time to see who it was, however, as the doors closed. Jane went to Mrs. Fairfax's room, but there was no Mrs. Fairfax. There was, however, a dog sitting on the rug. It was the dog from the lane. Jane called his name—"Pilot"—and the dog reacted. Jane did not know where he had come from. Leah, the servant, entered. Jane asked her where the dog had come from. Leah replied it had come with his master, Mr. Rochester, who had just arrived. He, Mrs Fairfax and Adele were in the dining room waiting until the doctor arrived to help with his ankle. Mrs. Fairfax entered a moment later to announce the surgeon had arrived, and Jane went to take off her things.

Chapter Thirteen:

Mr. Rochester went to bed early that night and did not rise again until later the next day. When he did, it was only due to business. His agent and some tenants had arrived and wanted to speak with him. Adele and Jane could not use the library anymore because it had to be used by Mr. Rochester for his business, so they ended up in an apartment upstairs. Thornfield was a changed place. It was no longer as quiet as a Church as every hour or so a knock at the door or a clang of the bell would come. There were more footsteps in the halls and more voices. Jane liked it. It was difficult to teach Adele as she could not focus on her studies. She kept running to the door to look over the bannisters to see Mr. Rochester and made up excuses for her to go downstairs. Jane got a little angry with her, but Adele only continued to chatter endlessly about the presents Mr. Rochester had suggested he had brought for her.

When the day turned dark, Jane allowed Adele to go downstairs as the silence indicated Mr. Rochester had had no more visitors. Jane sat by the fireplace until Mrs. Fairfax came in and asked if she and Adele would have tea with Mr. Rochester in the drawing room. She told Jane she had to change her dress before she went down, which surprised Jane. Mrs. Fairfax gave her a brooch to wear, and then they went down. She followed Mrs. Fairfax closely. Pilot and Adele sat near the fire. Mr. Rochester sat with his foot supported on a cushion. Jane's previous estimation of Mr. Rochester was a sound one: his characteristics were quite grim and serious, and his figure was quite square and athletic. Although Mr. Rochester must have been aware of their entrance, he did not look like he was in the mood to notice them.

Mrs. Fairfax presented Jane to him. He bowed, but did not look away from Adele. He told Mrs. Fairfax that Jane should sit down. Jane did not care that he was disinterested: it was easier for her than Mr. Rochester treating her with extreme kindness. Mr. Rochester did not speak or move, even though Mrs. Fairfax talked through the silence. The only thing he did say was to ask for tea. When it arrived, Mrs. Fairfax asked Jane to hand Mr. Rochester his cup, as Adele might have spilled it. Adele began asking for a present for Jane. Mr. Rochester challenged Jane and asked if she had expected a present, or if she liked them. Jane knew that they were nice things to receive, but had not had much experience with them. Mr. Rochester accused Jane of avoiding answering the question. Jane did not know why she would expect a present from Mr. Rochester considering that they were strangers. Mr. Rochester told her off for being too modest. He was pleased with the progress Adele had made even though she had no real talents or intelligence. Jane thanked him for the present of a compliment, but Mr. Rochester huffed and went quiet. After the tea was finished, Mr. Rochester asked Adele and Jane to come closer to the fire.

Jane discussed her past with Mr. Rochester. He was amazed that she spent eight years at Lowood as he would have thought that half that time would have been enough. He thinks this explains her far away look. When he came across her in the road, he had been reminded of fairy tales, and thought she had cast a spell on his horse. Mr. Rochester joked that she had probably been waiting for spirits when she sat on the stile. Jane joined in with his talk of fairy tales, but Mrs. Fairfax was a little concerned by their conversation.

Mrs. Fairfax stood up for Jane and told Mr. Rochester that she had been a great addition to the house, but he only wanted to judge her for himself, especially as she made his horse fall over. They discussed how much Jane had read, and whether or not she looked up to Mr. Brocklehurst. Jane did not like him one bit. She told Mr. Rochester that he starved them, cut off their hair, and did not buy them good enough needles and thread with which to sew their clothes. He asked if she could play the piano. Jane admitted she could play a little, and so Mr. Rochester ordered her to go and play a little for them. Before she did, he told her to wait and to forgive him for his tone of voice. He told her to stop after a moment—he admitted that she could play a little, but not much more than average people could. Jane closed the piano and returned to him.

He asked about some of her sketches which Adele had shown him, and suggested that she could not have possibly drawn them herself. Jane assured him she did, and he suggested that she was too proud, and that she should fetch her portfolio to prove to him that she had talent. Jane fetched her portfolio for him, and they looked at them one by one. He set three aside, and swept the rest away from him. He asked when she found time to draw. She drew them during her vacation time at Lowood, and did not copy them from other pictures but imagined them in her head. Mr. Rochester stared at them again: they were water colours of a swollen sea, a hill at night and an iceberg. He wondered if she was happy when she painted them, and if she was satisfied. Jane was not satisfied with them as they did not match what she aimed to do. Mr. Rochester disagreed: he thought that she managed to paint them very well, but they were strange images for a schoolgirl. He did not understand how she managed to think up these kind of images or how she learned to draw the way she did. Jane put her paintings away and then Mr. Rochester exclaimed at the time — it was time Adele ought to be in bed. Adele went to kiss him before she left, but he did not seem to want her to. He gestured as if he was tired of their company — Mrs. Fairfax put away her knitting, Jane fetched her portfolio and they all left.

Jane commented to Mrs. Fairfax that Mr. Rochester was quite abrupt and changed his moods often. Mrs. Fairfax was used to it — it was in his nature, and he could not help being the way he was. He had painful thoughts and family troubles, especially after he lost his elder brother nine years prior. Jane wondered if they were very close for Mr. Rochester to be still affected by his loss. Mrs. Fairfax didn't think they were. She knew that his father was not particularly kind to his son and put him in a difficult position so that he could earn his fortune without splitting the family property up between two sons. Mrs. Fairfax never knew what the exact situation was, but he separated himself from his family and lived in an unsettled way. She did not think he had lived at Thornfield for a fortnight at a time. She thought that he shunned Thornfield because it was gloomy looking. Jane wanted a clearer answer, but Mrs. Fairfax could not give her any specifics.

Chapter Fourteen:

For the next several days, Jane saw little of Mr. Rochester. He was consumed with business in the morning, and visitors in the afternoon how often stayed to have dinner with him. When his sprain had healed, he rode his horse often, but Jane did not know where to. Adele was hardly ever called into his presence, and so Jane only ever saw Mr. Rochester when they passed one another in the hall. He would acknowledge her presence with a curt nod or glance. Sometimes he would smile at her. His mood changes did not affect her too much as she had nothing to do with affection them. One day he had company at dinner and he sent for Jane's portfolio to look at.

When they left, Mr. Rochester called for Adele and Jane to come downstairs. Adele wondered if her present had finally come, and was grateful to see it sitting on the dining room table. Mr. Rochester sarcastically told her to enjoy it, but quietly. Mr. Rochester asked Jane to come and sit closer. He told her not to move the chair further away, and then chastised himself for ordering her around again. He did not want to listen to Adele talking about her presents, so called for Mrs. Fairfax to join them. Jane preferred to stay in the shade, but Mr. Rochester would not have her move the chair. He did not look as gloomy as he had before, and even had a smile on his face. After two minutes of observing him, Mr. Rochester asked if she thought he was handsome. Jane thought she should have considered the answer before she opened her mouth, but she told him she did not think he was handsome. When he observed that her answer had been quite a blunt one, she apologized and asked him for forgiveness. She explained that tastes differ and that beauty had little importance to her.

He did not accept her explanation and pushed her to tell him what faults she found in him. Jane asked if they could forget her first answer, but Mr. Rochester wanted her to criticize him. He pointed to his forehead and asked her if he was a fool. Jane did not think he was, but asked if he considered himself a philanthropist. Mr. Rochester agreed he was not in the general sense of the word, particularly as he could not stand the company of children and old women, but did have a conscience. He once had a tender, kind heart too, but that was kicked out of him. He wondered if he was capable of being transformed back — if he could regain his heart. Jane did not know what answer to give him and assumed he had drank too much wine. Mr. Rochester liked the way Jane looked when she was deep in thought, especially if it kept her from staring at him. He announced he was in the mood to talk, and then stood.

He was determined to learn more about Jane, and wanted her to speak. Jane did not know what he wanted her to talk about, so kept quiet. He, once again, apologized for treating her like an inferior, but suggested that he was more advanced than her because of his age and experience. Jane liked that he felt he needed to apologize, but still could not think of what to say. She suggested he should ask her questions. Mr. Rochester asked if she agreed with his right to be masterful. While Jane avoids answering the question directly at first, Mr. Rochester pushes her to admit that she disagrees with him. His claim of superiority only depends on how he has used his time and experience, not that he has gained it. He asked if he could deliver orders without insulting her. Jane thought he was strange for asking if a paid employee minded being ordered around. Mr. Rochester had forgotten that he was paying her. Jane was impressed that he cared about the feelings of a dependent

He commented that her view was a unique one, but told her not to take this as a compliment. It was only due to her nature that she ended up the way she had. Jane thought that he had his own flaws, too, and Mr. Rochester seemed to hear her thoughts and admit as much himself. He envied Jane for her clear conscience. Jane wondered if he did not remember being eighteen if he felt this way. Mr. Rochester assured her he was not a villain, but not a good man. He thinks that others will confide in her the way he has when she grows older. Jane doesn't know how he has reached this conclusion.

The conversation moves to an exploration of repentance and forgiveness. Jane believes it is right to forgive, but Mr. Rochester thinks that he should seek happiness, even at the expense of others. It is owed to him considering his awful life. Jane argues that he will grow sadder if he does this, especially if his happiness costs him something. When Mr. Rochester argues that she has no right to lecture him, Jane reminds him of his own words: he was the one to argue that sin brought the need for forgiveness and remorse, and that remorse was a poison to people.

After a confusing turn in the conversation, Jane brings them both back to the matter at hand. She argues that if he tried hard to better himself, he would be more approving of himself. Mr. Rochester agrees that he has the intention and hope he will be a better person. When Mr. Rochester suggests that he has the ability to decide his actions are right, much in the same way that God can, Jane stands and announces she has to take Adele to bed. Mr. Rochester accuses her of being afraid. Jane insists she just doesn't want to talk nonsense with him. He thinks Lowood's influence on her means she is restricted. He argues that Jane is afraid of smiling too much or speaking freely in the presence of a man, but insists she will get used to him soon. He thinks she is trapped, like a caged bird, and that a vibrant, restless person lives inside Jane.

But Jane still wants to leave. Mr. Rochester informs her that Adele, after unwrapping her new dress, had already left with Sophie to try it on. He predicts she will step back inside, the spitting image of her mother, Celine Varens. Adele enters, as predicted. She dances across the room, spins in front of Mr. Rochester and goes down to one knee. Mr. Rochester admits that Adele's mother charmed money out of his pocket, and left him with Adele, whom he would rather be rid of on some days. He wishes them all good night.

Chapter Fifteen:

Mr. Rochester told Jane about Adele one afternoon in the gardens. Celine Varens was a French opera-dancer, and they had great passion for one another. He was very flattered by her interest in him that he paid for a hotel room, gave her servants, a carriage, clothes and diamonds. He started to ruin himself financially. He visited one evening and found that Celine was out. He decided to sit and wait for her out on the balcony. He saw Celine's carriage pull up outside and was just about to call out for her when a cloaked figure wearing a hat stepped out behind her. Mr. Rochester wondered for a moment if Jane had ever felt jealousy, and then decided she hadn't — she had never been in love, surely. He changed the subject momentarily, to tell her he likes Thornfield, but had hated and shunned it for so long. He begins to tell her he hates it almost as something else, but does not take the subject any further. Instead, he descended into silence and glared at the battlements above them. He broke the silence to tell Jane he was arranging a deal with Destiny. He wanted to like Thornfield, and she dared him to do so. Mr. Rochester repeats his desire to be a good man.

Jane brought him back to the subject of Celine Varens and asked if he left the balcony. He had forgotten they were talking about her. He thought it was strange that he had chosen to confide in Jane, and that she — a young lady — listened quietly to him as if it was normal subject for an inexperienced girl to hear. He did not think he could negatively influence Jane, though, as her mind was a unique one. He stayed in the balcony, aiming to ambush them. He drew the curtain across so that there was only a small opening he could see through and waited for them. Celine and the soldier entered the room. Mr. Rochester's jealousy disappeared as soon as he saw them both because his love for Celine disappeared too. He could not love someone who could so easily betray him. Celine and the soldier began to talk about Mr. Rochester after seeing his calling card on the table. They both insulted him, and Celine discussed his "deformities". Adele ran up to Mr. Rochester and interrupted the story to let him know a businessman had arrived to see him. Mr. Rochester decided to skip some of the story. He walked in on Celine and the soldier, refused to pay for Celine anymore and told her to leave the hotel immediately. He ignored her plea for help.

The following day he shot the soldier in the arm, and thought he was finished with all of them. Unfortunately, Adele had been born six months prior, and Celine insisted that she was his daughter. Mr. Rochester still doubted this. A few years after they broke up, Celine abandoned Adele and ran away to Italy. He did not acknowledge Adele as his daughter, but still took her out of the slums of Paris and brought her to England. Mr. Rochester wondered if Jane would wish for another governess to be hired now that she knew the child was the offspring of a French opera-dancer. Jane rejected this argument: Adele was not responsible for anyone else's faults, and she was fond of Adele. She vowed to cling closer to Adele now that she knew the child was essentially an orphan.

Mr. Rochester went back inside the house. Jane stayed with Adele and Pilot and played a few games with her. When they went in, Jane allowed Adele to sit on her knee and talk endlessly for an hour, even when she descended into the trivial. Jane did not see a single thing in Adele that reminded her of Mr. Rochester, which she thought was a shame. If there had been anything of a resemblance, Mr. Rochester might have liked her a little more. Jane did not focus on Mr. Rochester's story until she went to bed that night. She thought there was something strange in Mr. Rochester's mood when he stared up at the battlements, but as she could not explain it she pushed the subject aside. She reflected that he seemed pleased to see her and talk to her lately, and Jane was honoured that she amused him. She did not speak much during their encounters, and let him speak endlessly, eager for his ideas and opinions. His easiness around her made her feel much more relaxed around him, and sometimes she felt that they could be members of the same family. She was happy to have him in her life. She liked to see his face, and his presence made her happy. She could not forget his faults—especially not when he insisted on bringing them up at every opportunity. He was also quite moody: Jane often found him slumped across the library table in a foul mood. Jane thought he was naturally better, but could not become his authentic self because of what had happened to him. She felt sorry for him and his past, whatever it was, and would have done a lot to help him if he could. She wondered what kept him from enjoying Thornfield, and if he would leave it again soon. He had stayed eight weeks when he rarely stayed more than two, and Jane dreaded the day he might go.

Jane began to hear strange murmurs. She sat up in bed, listening, but the sound had disappeared. She heard someone in the hall, but when Jane asked who was there, no one answered. Jane considered that it might be Pilot wandering the halls, which calmed her down. Just as Jane was about to fall asleep, she heard a demonic laugh from the hall. Jane looked around but could not see anyone in her room. The laugh came again, and Jane went to the hall and cried out. Steps retreated toward the third storey staircase. She wondered if it was Grace Poole again, and if she had been possessed. She decided to go to Mrs. Fairfax. Jane was surprised that the air was full of smoke, and she could smell burning. Mr. Rochester's door was slightly ajar and the smoke was coming from his room. She stepped into the room, all thoughts of Grace and Mrs. Fairfax gone. The curtains around the bed were on fire!

Mr. Rochester was sound asleep. Jane shook him to try and wake him up, but he only turned over. She ran to his water basin and poured water over the bed and Mr. Rochester. She then ran to her own room and fetched the water jug, returning to the bed to drench it and put the fire out. Mr. Rochester finally woke up. He asked if there was a flood. Jane replied there had been a fire, and that she would fetch a candle for them. Mr. Rochester wondered if Jane was trying to drown him, and if she was a witch. Jane told him to get up as someone had tried to kill him and they needed to find out who. He pulled his dressing gown on as she fetched a candle, and showed him the burned bed. Jane told him the story of the demonic laugh and the steps near the third storey steps. She wondered if she had to fetch Mrs. Fairfax or one of the other servants, but Mr. Rochester wanted to let them sleep. He wrapped his cloak around her and told her to sit in the armchair in the corner. He ordered her to sit still, not move and wait for him to return for her. He left her in the dark.

Just as Jane did not think there was any point in staying, Mr. Rochester returned. He told her that he had found out what had happened, and that it was exactly as he feared. He wondered if she had seen anything else beside the candles, and if she had heard the laughs before. Jane had heard the laughter—it was Grace Poole. Mr. Rochester agreed it was her. He told Jane not to say anything about the incident and to go back to bed. Jane stood and said good night. Mr. Rochester wondered why she was leaving without them saying anything about the fact that she had saved his life. He told her they had to at least shake hands. They did. Mr. Rochester told her he owed her a great debt, but did not feel the burden of that debt. He almost said something else, but stopped himself before he did. Jane assured him he owed her no debt. He was sure that she would do him some good at some point in his life—he had seen it in her eyes when they first met. He wished his preserver a good night, but did not let go of her hands. Jane told him she must go as she was cold, but he still didn't let go of her. Jane told him she heard Mrs. Fairfax moving about, and Mr. Rochester let go of her hands.

Jane returned to her bed but she could not sleep. As she imagined the sea and lands beyond it she would never reach, she assured herself that sound judgement would keep her passion in check.

Chapter Sixteen:

Jane wanted but feared seeing Mr. Rochester the next morning. She wanted to hear his voice, but was afraid to meet his eye. She expected him to visit the schoolroom, as he sometimes did, but he did not. Nothing interrupted her class with Adele. Just after breakfast, she heard Mrs. Fairfax, Leah and a few others talking in Mr. Rochester's chamber. They were glad that Mr. Rochester had not burnt to death in his sleep, that he had quickly worked to put the fire out, and were surprised he had kept a candle burning at night. She heard them putting the chamber back in order, and when she walked by later on saw that everything was tidied and clean. Jane was about to ask Leah, who was washing the windows, what had happened when she saw Grace Poole herself sitting in the corner and sewing rings to new curtains. She did not look upset at all. She wished Jane a good morning, as she usually did, and then went back to her sewing. Jane decided to test her by asking what had happened.

Grace told her that Mr. Rochester had fallen asleep while reading the previous night, and the candle had lit the curtains on fire. Jane asked if he had woken anyone up. Grace examined her carefully before answering that the servants slept too far away to hear noises and Mrs. Fairfax did not hear as well as she used to. She asked Jane if she had heard anything. Jane told her quietly that she had heard a laugh. Grace did not react. She did not think Mr. Rochester would have laughed if he had been in danger, and concluded that Jane must have been dreaming. Jane insisted she was not. Grace asked if she had told Mr. Rochester about the laugh, and if she had looked out into the hall. Jane was suddenly aware that Grace was looking for information herself and feared that she might be the next target. Jane told her she bolted her door. Grace concluded that Jane did not bolt her door every night. Jane thought Grace wanted to know her habits so she could plan properly. Jane assured her that in the future she would lock her door every night. Grace told her it was wise to do so just in case any trouble emerged in the house, quiet though it was. Jane was amazed by her hypocrisy. The cook stepped in and asked if Grace was coming down to eat with the other servants. She asked for it to be put on a tray so she could take it upstairs. Jane left when she heard Mrs. Fairfax was waiting for her.

Jane hardly heard Mrs. Fairfax talk as she considered Grace Poole's odd behaviour and wondering why she had not been arrested that morning, or even dismissed from service. Mr. Rochester had essentially told Jane that Grace was guilty the previous night, but she did not know what kept him from accusing her in public. It was strange considering that Mr. Rochester was such a commanding man in other respects. If Grace had been pretty and young, Jane might have suspected that this had an influence on Mr. Rochester, but she was hard and matronly. She wondered if they had a past indiscretion which Grace held over Mr. Rochester. She did not dare to agree with this thought, but she could not completely disregard it. Jane thought she was not beautiful either, and Mr. Rochester seemed to like her a great deal. She remembered the way he looked at her and talked the previous night.

As evening approached, Jane realized she had not heard Mr. Rochester speak or walk around in the house that day. She expected to see him in the evening. Even though she had initially worried about meeting with him again, her impatience to see him overrode any fear. Adele left to go and play with Sophie in the nursery, and Jane listened for the bell to ring, or for Leah to fetch her. Sometimes she thought she heard Mr. Rochester outside in the hall and turned, expecting to open the door to admit him in, but the door remained shut. She wanted to ask him about Grace Poole and see what he would say. Leah did come, finally, but only to tell her that Mrs. Fairfax was waiting for her in her room. Jane joined her for tea. Mrs. Fairfax was afraid that Jane was feeling sick, but she assured Mrs. Fairfax she was feeling fine. Mrs. Fairfax commented that the weather had been good for Mr. Rochester's journey that day.

Jane was surprised. She wondered where he had gone, and how long he would be gone for. He had joined a group of friends, and Mrs. Fairfax did not expect him to return for a week or so. Gentlemen rarely wanted to leave one when they were entertained. Mrs. Fairfax thought the ladies were quite fond of Mr. Rochester, and there were at least three elegant young ladies present at this gathering. One, in particular, had caught Mr. Rochester's eye: a Miss Ingram. She was very beautiful and sang a duet with Mr. Rochester at their last gathering. Jane wondered why she had not been married yet, and if Mr. Rochester would marry her. Mrs. Fairfax did not think they would because of the age difference — Miss Ingram was almost fifteen years younger. Jane did not think this was a large difference, but Mrs. Fairfax insisted Mr. Rochester would not consider it.

When she was alone again, Jane looked into her own heart to examine her thoughts and feelings. She had been cherishing and reliving the pleasant moments with Mr. Rochester for the past few weeks, and ignored the reality of her situation. She told herself off for thinking she might be important to Mr. Rochester at all. She did not think it was good that her superior would flatter her when he had no interest in marrying her. Her punishment would be to look in the mirror the next morning and to draw herself as realistically as possible, defects and all. Next, she would take the loveliest paints and draw her impression of Miss Blanch Ingram. In the future, if she considered that Mr. Rochester might care for her, she would have to compare both of the pictures and tell herself he would never waste a serious thought on her over Miss Ingram.

She kept her word, and after a few weeks had a portrait of both herself and the imaginary Blanche Ingram. Jane liked the task — it gave her self-control and focus. She was able to approach future events with a calm she did not think she would have possessed prior to the exercise.

Chapter Seventeen:

Ten days passed without any news from Mr. Rochester. Mrs. Fairfax said she would not be surprised if he went straight to London, and then to Europe. He probably would not visit Thornfield for another year. It was not the first time he had left the house so abruptly, and Jane was afraid that she was feeling disappointed about it. She pulled herself together and told herself that she had nothing to do with him at all, except to receive her salary from him and teach his ward. She went on with her day as usual but every now and then had passing thoughts regarding why she should leave Thornfield. She tried to keep these thoughts away from her.

After two weeks they finally received post from Mr. Rochester. Mrs. Fairfax read the letter quietly over breakfast. Jane turned hot and spilled her coffee — she did not know why, and she did not want to think what the reasons might be. Mrs. Fairfax suggested that they would be busy again for a little while. Jane asked for an explanation but tried not to draw too much attention to her interest. Mrs. Fairfax revealed that he was due to return to Thornfield in three days and was bringing someone with him. She did not know how many of their group would return with him, but he had sent orders for all the best bedrooms to be cleaned out, and to hire on more servants. They will have a full house. Mrs. Fairfax went away to start preparations.

The next three days were very busy ones. Jane had thought that the rooms were very clean, but she was mistaken. Three women were hired to scrub, wash, beat carpets, move pictures, polish and airing out the linen. Adele went into a frenzy herself, and asked Sophie to look over her dresses, to get rid of the ones that were not fit for society and to air out the ones she could wear. She jumped off furniture, lay on piled up mattresses and ran wild. She did not have to sit with Jane for lessons as Jane was pulled into the kitchen to help. Jane thought she might be hindering them rather than helping them, but they still managed to bake custard, cheesecakes, pastries and to dress dishes. They were expecting the group to arrive in time for dinner on the Thursday, and Jane had little time to consider her true feelings about Mr. Rochester's return. Every now and then Jane would be struck with a sudden bout of sadness.

One day, she looked at the third storey staircase door, which had been locked all the time recently, and saw Grace Poole emerge from it. She would only spend one hour out of every twenty four with the other servants as the rest of the time she spent sewing in private. Jane thought it was very strange that no one else seemed to notice her odd habits or hours, and no one ever pitied Grace for her isolation. She did, however, overhear a conversation between Leah and one of the other servants regarding Grace one day. They discussed her wages, which were very high. Leah thought she would have had enough saved by then to be an independent woman and not work any more, but she guessed Grace stayed because she wasn't forty yet and was used to Thornfield. When the other servant asked if Grace was good at what she did, Leah agreed that she knew what she had to do and that no one else could do what she did. When the servant was about to say something else, Leah nudged her, having noticed Jane listening in. Jane heard the servant whisper a question: she wondered if Jane knew. Leah said she didn't, and the conversation was dropped. Jane knew then that there was a mystery at Thornfield which she knew nothing about.

When Thursday came, all the preparation work had been finished. Mrs. Fairfax put on one of her best gowns as she would be greeting the group of guests. Adele had dressed up too, but Jane thought she had little chance of meeting them that day. Jane did not change her own clothes as she would not leave her sanctuary of the schoolroom. She sat at the open window that evening working. Mrs. Fairfax stepped in and looked out the window for John, whom she had sent to the gate to see if the group were on their way. John had returned and told them that they were about to arrive in ten minutes. Adele flew to the window, and Jane stood close by, but hid herself behind the curtain. After a long ten minutes, two open carriages arrived with riders on horses close by. Mr. Rochester and a lady dressed in purple rode side by side on horses. Mrs. Fairfax recognized her immediately: this was Miss Ingram! Mrs. Fairfax hurried to meet them as the carriage pulled out of their sight. Adele begged to go down to meet them. Jane sat her on her knee and told her not to expect to be in the ladies' company any time soon. She would have to wait to be sent for by Mr. Rochester, or he might be angry with her. Adele cried a little, but Jane gave her a serious look until she wiped her face.

The sound of the gentlemen and ladies in the hall gave way for Mr. Rochester's voice. They walked up the stairs, through the hall and went into various rooms. Adele followed every noise carefully and knew that they were getting ready for dinner. Jane wondered if Adele was hungry and decided to go and fetch her something to eat while the ladies were in their rooms. She took the back staircase down to the busy, bustling kitchen, and found some food for them to eat. She had just reached the hall when the noise from the rooms indicated the ladies were about to leave. She did not want to be caught by them, and could not go to the schoolroom without passing some of their doors. She stood in the dark at the other end of the hall while the ladies left the room one by one almost noiselessly. Jane was struck by their elegance. Jane found Adele peeping through the schoolroom door, hoping that Mr. Rochester would ask for them to come down after the dinner. Jane told Adele not to get her hopes up, and that he might see them tomorrow. He had other things on his mind instead. Jane allowed Adele to sit up far longer than she normally did because there was no chance of her getting to sleep with footmen running to and from the kitchen with trays. Besides, Adele still hoped that she might be called downstairs. Jane told her stories for as long as she would listen to them, and then took her out into the hallway. It amused Adele to watch the servants walking back and forth.

Later on in the evening, the sound of a piano started up. Adele and Jane sat at the top of the stairs to listen to a lady singing alongside the piano. Once the solo was over, a duet followed, and then the group descended into chatter once more. Jane discovered that she was intently listening for Mr. Rochester's voice among the others and trying to figure out what he might be saying. When the clock struck eleven, Jane took Adele to bed, but it was near one in the morning before the party went to bed.

The next day's weather was nice enough for the party to go out into the neighbourhood. Jane saw the departure and their return to Thornfield. Miss Ingram was, again, the only lady riding a horse, and again rode beside Mr. Rochester. Jane pointed this out to Mrs. Fairfax and observed that they might be married. Mrs. Fairfax admitted that he admired her. Jane wished she had actually seen Miss Ingram's face at some point. Mrs. Fairfax was certain that Jane would see her face that very night. She had told Mr. Rochester that Adele wanted to meet the ladies, and he had agreed to invite both her and Jane into the drawing room after dinner. Jane thought Mr. Rochester had only invited her out of politeness and did not want to go, but Mrs. Fairfax told her she had said exactly the same to Mr. Rochester, and he had demanded Jane join them. If she did not, he would go and fetch her himself. Jane agreed to go to save him the trouble, but did not want to go. Mrs. Fairfax admitted that she was not going herself and gave Jane some advice. She would have to go into the drawing room while it was empty so that she could find a quiet corner to sit in so that no one would notice her. She could then leave just after the gentlemen arrived unless she wanted to stay. Jane asked if the party would stay long. Mrs. Fairfax didn't think they would stay any longer than three weeks as many of them had other business to attend to.

Adele spent most of the day in great excitement, but Jane dreaded the visit to the drawing room. It was only once Adele was formally dressed that she calmed down. When she was ready, she took care to not crease her dress and assured Jane she would not move an inch until they were ready to leave. Jane put her best dress on and then took Adele downstairs. They went into the empty drawing room. There was a curtain that separated the drawing room from the salon where the party were eating dinner, but Jane could not hear their distinct conversation. Adele sat on a footstool very quietly while Jane read at a window seat. Adele asked if she might have a flower to improve her appearance. Jane scolded Adele for thinking too much about her appearance, but gave her one to slip into her sash. Now happy, Adele sighed. Finally the curtain was swept back, revealing the group of ladies. There were only eight of them, but they gave Jane the impression that there were far more of them because of the length of their dresses and their tall heights. Jane stood up to curtsey to them, but only one or two nodded at her. The rest stared. They floated to various places around the room, reminding Jane of a flock of birds.

Jane knew their names and revealed them. Mrs. Eshton and her two daughters, Amy and Louisa, were quite pretty. Lady Lynn was a large, snooty looking woman. Mrs. Colonel Dent was not dressed as extravagantly as Lady Lynn, but Jane thought she looked more like a lady. The Dowager Lady Ingram and her two daughters, Blanche and Mary, were the most distinguished of the group. Although they were very well dressed, Jane thought they also looked quite self important. Jane was more interested in Blanche than anyone else there, for obvious reasons. She wanted to see if Mrs. Fairfax's description of her had been correct, if it was similar to Jane's own painting and to see if Jane herself would be likely to suit Mr. Rochester's taste. She was similar to both the painting and to Mrs. Fairfax's description, but did not reflect the same personality Jane had expected. Miss Ingram was self conscious and played on other people's ignorance. Her sister, Mary, was not like her — she had softer features, said nothing and had an expressionless face.

Jane could not tell if Miss Ingram was a good match for Mr. Rochester or not, but she guessed that many men admired her, but she wanted more proof. This proof would come when she saw them together. While Jane had been admiring the ladies, Adele had stood up to welcome them all. Miss Ingram mocked Adele by calling her a puppet. Mrs. Dent and the two Eshton sisters were the only ones to welcome Adele with warmth and took her to a sofa to talk to her. When coffee was brought in, Jane remained half hidden. The men were tall and well dressed. Jane tried to avoid looking for Mr. Rochester, but still saw him enter the room. She tried to focus on her knitting in her hands and to only saw it, but memories of the last time she saw him entered her mind. They had stood close to one another on the night he had almost died, and she wondered what had happened since then to change their positions. She did not even expect him to speak to her. He sat on the other side of the room and talked to the ladies there. When Jane knew he was distracted she looked up involuntarily to look at him. It gave her pleasure to see him. She thought he was beautiful. She had not intended on falling in love with him, but on seeing him again knew that she was. She quietly compared him to the other gentlemen in the room and, although she knew many would find them attractive, only had eyes for Mr. Rochester. He was talking to Louisa and Amy Eshton, and Jane was amazed that neither of the girls reacted to the intense looks Mr. Rochester gave them. She realized that neither of them liked him as much as she did. Jane considered that she and Mr. Rochester might be suited after all, even though she had told herself only a few days before that she was only allowed to think of him as her employer. Jane once again reminded herself that she had to push away her hope even though she could not deny her love for him.

While the conversation flows over coffee, Jane watches them all. Miss Ingram was the only person without a companion, and she walked over to Mr. Rochester to talk to him. They discussed Adele; Miss Ingram wanted her to be sent to school, but Mr. Rochester could not afford it. Miss Ingram pointed out that he had enough money to pay for a governess. Jane wondered if he would look over at her, but he stared straight ahead. Miss Ingram declared she detested all the governesses she had when she was younger, and her mother was glad she no longer had to deal with them. They refer to Jane as a prime example of everything wrong with governesses. Mr. Rochester asks them what the faults are. Blanche admits that she never suffered under their protection as she made sure to play tricks on them. Her father remembers those days; one governess in particular called the children villains, and he lectured her for attempting to teach his clever children when she was so stupid herself. Amy Eshton stepped into the conversation, then, and told them their own governess was never cross with them, even when they tried to trick her. Miss Ingram sarcastically commented that they would now have to hear endless stories about governesses and asked to change the subject. Mr. Rochester agreed.

Miss Ingram decided she would play for them, and wondered who might join her. The group agreed that Mr. Rochester should join her for the song. Blanche played around on the piano for a moment, ranting about men of the present day. If she married a man, he would have to be more in love with her than his own image. She announced that an ugly woman was a horrible sight, but a gentleman obsessed with the way he looked was just as bad. She told Mr. Rochester to sing while she played. They exchanged a playful banter: Mr. Rochester suggested he might sing poorly for her, Blanche told him to sing. Jane thought she might slip away from the group, then, but Mr. Rochester's lovely singing voice froze her in place. She waited until he had finished, then stood and walked out of the nearby side-door. In the hall she found her shoe was untied and bent to tie it. The dining room door opened, and Mr. Rochester stepped out. He asked her why she did not speak to him. Jane thought she might have asked the same question of him, but only answered that he seemed engaged with the group. Mr. Rochester observed that she was paler, and wondered if she had caught a cold. She denied she was sick. Mr. Rochester told her to go back into the drawing room. She was leaving far too early. Jane told him she was tired. Mr. Rochester thought she was depressed, too, and asked her what was the matter. He did not believe her—she was close to crying after only a few words between them. If there was no threat of a servant walking in on them, he might have pressed for more information. He allowed her to go to her room, but she would have to be in the drawing room every night until his visitor's left. Just as Mr. Rochester wished her a good night, he almost called her by an affectionate name and stopped himself before he did.

Chapter Eighteen:

All of Jane's sad feelings about the house had disappeared. She was not restless anymore because the house was so full of life. Even the weather was beautiful. One of the first nights in the drawing room, the guests and Mr. Rochester played Charades. The servants ran up and downstairs bringing costumes and other items into the drawing room to be used. Mr. Rochester paired himself off with Blanche. He asked if Jane would play, but she shook her head. She worried that he would force her to play, but he allowed her to go and sit quietly. One of the gentlemen asked Lady Ingram if they should ask Jane to join the game, but she said Jane was far too stupid to play it.

Mr. Rochester's group went behind a curtain to prepare for their part of the game. The curtain rose to reveal a wedding party. Mr. Rochester and Miss Ingram pretended to walk down the aisle together and kneel. Colonel Dent's party talked for a few moments and then called out "Bride" as the answer. Two more scenes came and went, with Mr. Rochester pretending to be in jail for the last. Miss Ingram complimented him on his acting and admitted she liked him in the last scene the best. Mr. Rochester teased her for wanting a bandit or criminal for her man, and jokingly reminded her that they had been married in front of the entire group just moments before. Colonel Dent's group took their turn to put on the small scenes for the game of charades but Jane did not remember a single one of them. She was too absorbed in watching Miss Ingram and Mr. Rochester together. She watched them whisper to one another and exchange glances.

Jane would often spend hours in Mr. Rochester's presence without him looking her way a single time, and she knew this was because Miss Ingram was in his presence. She was a great lady, and Jane thought they would be married soon. Jane was not jealous, even though she knew that this situation would usually make anyone jealous. Jane did not think Miss Ingram deserved her jealousy. She was below it. She was not a genuine person and had no real love. Jane saw her spitefulness in the way she treated Adele as an insect. She ordered the girl from the room sometimes and treated her with coldness. Mr. Rochester even watched her do this, and Jane knew that he was well aware of Miss Ingram's faults. It upset Jane to know that the marriage would be a loveless one. Mr. Rochester was probably marrying her because her rank and fortune suited him, not because he loved her. It did not help Jane one bit. If Mr. Rochester had laid his heart at Miss Ingram's feet, Jane would have turned her face away. If Miss Ingram had been a good and noble woman, Jane would have admired her and kept quiet in the knowledge that Mr. Rochester had married her superior. Watching Miss Ingram repeatedly try to charm Mr. Rochester and seeing her fail and not actually realize it excited Jane to no end. Jane thought she might have done better if she had sat by his side, said less and looked less often at him. She did not think that she would be able to manage to keep him happy when they were married. Jane was surprised to conclude that Mr. Rochester would aim to marry for connections and money. She thought that he would not be the kind of man to be driven by these kinds of motives, but the longer she considered their class and childhoods, the more she realized that this kind of approach to marriage had been instilled in them since they were small.

Jane realized she was also ignoring Mr. Rochester's faults, which she had watched for originally so that she could have a well informed idea of his true nature. She would even miss his sarcasm and harsh judgement if he lost these qualities. She wanted to know Mr. Rochester's inner thoughts and unpack his mystery, and Jane thought Miss Ingram was happy because she would one day have the ability to do just that. Most of the guests busied themselves with activities, but they generally followed the direction of Mr. Rochester and Miss Ingram, who were the life of the party. If one or both of them were missing from the room, the people in it became dull and bored.

One day Mr. Rochester had to go to Millcote for business and was not likely to return to Thornfield until later. The group decided to go on a walk to a gypsy camp, but when the weather turned wet the group decided to stay in. It was almost dusk when Mr. Rochester returned in a carriage. Miss Ingram startled, standing up. She did not know why he had left on his own horse and returned in a carriage. She walked toward the window Jane sat beneath to look out. Jane curled her body back to try and hide, but Miss Ingram saw her anyway and moved to another window after sneering at her. The man who stepped out of the carriage was not Mr. Rochester at all, but a man in travelling clothes. Miss Ingram told Adele she was a monkey and glared at Jane, as if it was her fault Mr Rochester had not arrived.

The new arrival stepped into the room and bowed to Lady Ingram, deciding that she was the eldest lady present. He apologized for the intrusion, but he had come to stay with Mr. Rochester, an old friend of his. He had been on a long journey and wanted to wait for him. He was polite, but his accent was unusual — not quite foreign, but not quite English, either. He was around Mr. Rochester's age, and was a generally handsome man with a tame look. Jane did not like the vacant look in his face. When Jane saw him again, she noticed that his eyes wandered without purpose, and his face had no commanding presence. He repelled her. Jane sat in her usual hiding place and compared him to Mr. Rochester: she thought there couldn't be more of a difference between a sleek goose and a fierce falcon. Jane thought that their friendship, old as he claimed it was, had to have been a strange one to bring two extremes together. Jane sometimes caught snippets of conversation between him and the other gentlemen in the room, but could really only hear Louisa and Mary fawn over the stranger and how handsome he was. To Jane's relief, the women were called over by one of the men to discuss their excursion to the gypsy camp. Jane could finally listen in on the conversation.

She learned that the stranger's name was Mr. Mason and that he had just arrived in England from the West Indies. It was there that he and Mr. Rochester had made friends. Jane knew that Mr. Rochester had travelled, but had thought that he had travelled in Europe, not elsewhere. Jane was considering this point when Mr. Mason asked for some more coal to be put on the fire. The footman who had brought the coal stopped to talk to Mr. Eshton for a moment and Jane overheard them refer to a troublesome woman they wanted to send away. Colonel Dent told them to stop for a moment while he asked the ladies for their opinion. He revealed that one of the gypsies had arrived at the house demanding to be brought before the group so that she might read their fortunes. Lady Ingram did not want an imposter to be encourage and asked her to be sent away. The footman explained that no one had been able to send her away: she had sat on a chair and refused to move until their fortunes were told. After discovering that she was an ugly old woman, one of the men declared she had to be a real sorceress and to send her in. Lady Ingram once again objected, but Blanche silenced her. She wanted her fortune told and sent the footman running to fetch her.

The footman returned without her. She did not want to come before them all at once. Each one of them had to go to a room by themselves and have their fortunes read one by one. Lady Ingram began to use this as evidence that the old lady was a waste of time, but Blanche told him to show the gypsy to the library. She wanted the woman to herself. The footman disappeared and then returned when she was settled in the library. She did not want to see any of the gentlemen, and would only see the young and single ladies. Miss Ingram decided to go first, despite her mother's pleas. Silence fell on the group. Fifteen minutes passed before she returned to the group. Blanche walked stiffly to her seat and did not say a thing until she was asked. Blanche told them not to ask what she had been told as the gypsy woman was an imposter and should be placed in the stocks the following day as previously suggested now that her passing fancy had been met. She then picked up a book and declined to say anything else.

Jane watched her for half an hour: she did not turn a page and her face grew darker over time. Jane did not think Blanche had heard anything she wanted to hear, and that she had — despite her declaration — thought the gypsy woman had more importance than previously stated. Mary, Amy and Louisa wanted to go and see the gypsy but did not want to go alone. After negotiations, the gypsy woman finally agreed to see the trio together. They returned to the drawing room after twenty minutes shrieking and giggling together. The gypsy woman had known things they had done in their childhood, described books and ornaments they had in their bedrooms and so on. She had then whispered to each one of them the name of the person they liked the best in the world and told them what they most wished for. The gentlemen asked for details about the last two points, but the girls only blushed in response.

Jane noticed that the footman still stood at the door. He told her that the gypsy woman knew of one more single woman in the house she had not seen and vowed not to leave until she had. He guessed that must be Jane, but did not know what to say to the gypsy. Jane decided to go as she was curious herself. She slipped out of the room unnoticed and closed the door behind her. The footman offered to stand in the hall outside the door for her, but Jane told him to return to the kitchen. Jane was not afraid.

Chapter Nineteen:

Jane stepped into the calm library. The gypsy wore a cloak and a bonnet. An extinguished candle stood on the table. The gypsy bent over the fire and read from a little black book, muttering the words to herself. She did not stop when Jane entered the room, and Jane guessed that she wanted to finish her paragraph. Jane felt very calm. The gypsy closed her book finally and looked up at her. She asked Jane if she wanted her fortune told. Jane did not care either way and warned the old lady that she did not have faith. The gypsy told her that she was cold, sick and silly and that she would prove it. Jane was cold because she was alone, she was sick because her love was kept away from her, and she was silly because despite her suffering, she would not step toward her waiting love. Jane replied that she could say that about anyone alone in a big house. They argued between themselves for a moment about finding more examples like Jane in other houses. Whereas Jane thought there would be many of her in houses like Thornfield, the gypsy thought that it would be difficult to find her one. The gypsy told Jane that happiness was within her reach and that she must reach for it herself.

After giving the gypsy some money, Jane held out her hand. The gypsy could not read her hand because there were few lines in it. She asked to read Jane's forehead. After examining her for a moment, the gypsy wondered aloud how Jane had felt when she stepped into the room, and what she thought when she sat by herself in the drawing room. Jane admitted she felt tired much of the time, but did not feel sad. The gypsy wondered what kept her happier. Jane had no true hopes for the future — only to save enough money to set up her own little school. When the gypsy mentioned that Jane sat in the window-seat, Jane accused her of finding this information out from one of the servants. The gypsy admitted that she knew Grace Poole. Jane knew that there was trickery involved, but the gypsy went on to ask if she thought of nothing else but her dream school. She wondered if there was someone she watched. Jane admitted she watched most of them, particularly when there was something of interest going on between a few people. The gypsy woman asked what she liked to hear. Jane admitted she did not have much of a choice in subject as they would generally discuss the same things: courtship and marriage. The gypsy accused her of lying — why else would she smile at the gentlemen. Jane interrupted and assured her she did not even know the gentlemen, let alone smile at them. The gypsy asked if she could say the same about Mr. Rochester. Jane did not know what she was talking about.

The gypsy mentioned that most of the tales regarding matrimony had involved Mr. Rochester lately, and that Jane must have considered he would be happily married soon. Jane did not exactly agree with this statement. The gypsy asked for clarification, but Jane would not give it. She had not come to discuss Mr. Rochester's impending marriage to Miss Ingram. The gypsy declared the marriage must be a happy one — or, at least, Miss Ingram would be happy with Mr. Rochester's fortune. She had told Miss Ingram something that had made her look quite serious and suggested that Mr. Rochester should watch out in case she found someone with a larger fortune; the gypsy, it seemed, had suggested Mr. Rochester was not as rich as Blanche had first thought. Jane insisted that she had not come to hear Mr. Rochester's fortune but her own. The gypsy told her that her own fortune was doubtful — each one of Jane's traits contradicted the other. There was happiness in her future but only if she reaches out for it herself and takes it. The gypsy asks to study Jane's forehead again. She sees that Jane holds onto reason and judgement above emotions and passion. Suddenly, the woman's voice changed. Jane stood up but did not leave. She looked back at the gypsy and studied the hand that reached out for the fire. It was not the hand of an old woman and wore a ring on a little finger that she had seen many times before. It was Mr. Rochester in disguise. Jane did not know why he had done what he had, but told him he had done well with the other ladies. With her, he had spoken nonsense and was not fair. He asked if she could forgive him. She did not know — she would try to forgive him, but what he did was not right. Jane had acted correctly the entire time, suspecting some sort of trickery, but had imagined Grace Poole might have been the gypsy. She had not even considered Mr. Rochester.

Jane wanted to go to bed, but Mr. Rochester asked her to stay for a moment longer and tell her what the people in the drawing room had said about his gypsy. Jane mentioned she could not stay long on account of the time, and then remembered Mr. Mason had arrived to see him. Mr. Rochester turned quite pale and gripped Jane's wrist tightly. Jane asked if he was well. Mr. Rochester told her he had been struck a blow. Jane made him sit down. Mr. Rochester took her hand in his own and gazed at her with a troubled face. He wished that he could be on an island with only Jane and nothing to trouble him. She offered him help, and he vowed he would ask for it if she could help. She fetched a glass of wine for him and looked in on them to see what Mr. Mason was doing. Mr. Rochester downed the glass of wine while Jane told him they were laughing and joking with Mr. Mason. Mr. Rochester was worried they had heard something strange, and then asked Jane a strange question: if his visitors came into the room and spat on him, what would she do? Jane would send them away from the room. He asked what she would do if they whispered to one another, looked at him coldly and then left the room one by one. Would she go with them? Jane would rather be with Mr. Rochester to comfort him as well as she could. Even if they banned Jane from seeing him, Jane would not care about the ban and still be his friend. Mr. Rochester told her to Mr. Mason quietly and whisper to him that Mr. Rochester wanted to see him. Jane delivered the message, sent him to the library and then went upstairs. After a while, Jane heard the group go to bed, and then Mr. Rochester tell Mr. Mason his room was nearby. Mr. Rochester's tone was a happy one, and Jane finally went to sleep satisfied.

Chapter Twenty:

Jane had forgotten to draw her curtains, so the bright full moon shone on her and woke her up. As she reached out to draw the curtain a scream broke through Thornfield. Jane froze in place. The sound had come from the third story where there was clearly a struggle taking place. Someone called for help, and then cried out Rochester's name. Someone ran down the hall, something fell and then there was silence. Jane put some clothes on while people in rooms around her stirred and looked out of their rooms. Some ran, others crowded together in groups and confusion reigned throughout. Colonel Dent declared he could not find Mr. Rochester as he was not in his bed. Mr. Rochester cried out to them from the end of the hall, having come down from the third storey. He told them to calm down. Miss Ingram grabbed his arm and asked what had happened. Mr. Rochester told them all to keep away from him or he would say something he regretted. Jane thought he looked dangerous, and that his eyes were sparking. Mr. Rochester made an effort to calm himself down and told them that a servant had had a nightmare and had been so immersed in it that she had a fit. He told them all to go back to their rooms or the servant would not calm down. He sarcastically told Miss Ingram she would probably declare herself above nightmares. He commanded them all back to their rooms.

Jane did not need a command and retreated, as unnoticed as she came. She did not, however, go to her room to go back to bed. She had heard the commotion directly above her room and knew that Mr. Rochester's tale was a false one. She dressed to be ready for an emergency and sat at the window-seat, but did not know what it was she waited for. In about an hour Thornfield was silent again. Jane considered lying down on her bed when someone knocked at the door. It was Mr. Rochester, asking if she was still up and dressed. He asked her to come out into the hall quietly. He asked her to bring a sponge and salts from her room, then followed Mr. Rochester to the third storey door, which he unlocked. He asked if the sight of blood made her sick, and then led her up the stairs holding her hand. Jane remembered the room from the tour Mrs. Fairfax took her on, but there was a tapestry that had been lifted up to reveal a door behind it. A snarling sound, like a dog, came from the open door. Mr. Rochester told her to wait a moment, and then went inside. Jane heard Grace Poole's voice. Mr. Rochester came back out of the second room and closed the door behind him. He led Jane to the other side of the bed where Mr. Mason sat on a chair, his arm soaked in blood. While Jane held the candle, Mr. Rochester cleaned Mr. Mason's face and used the salts to wake him up. He then opened Mr. Mason's shirt to sponge away any blood. Mr. Rochester assured him that he had not been hurt badly, and he hoped Mr. Mason would be able to leave by the next morning. He asked Jane to stay with the man for the next hour or so and sponge away any blood. He ordered her not to speak to him, and for him to keep quiet. Mr. Rochester left the room.

Jane worried about Grace Poole coming into the room to try and kill her, but knew she had to keep to her post and watch over Mr. Mason. The tapestry of a dying Christ and Judas frightened her, too. Jane wondered what sort of creature lived inside the woman's body in the next room, and what kind of mystery had taken over the house, and how Mr. Mason—this stranger to the house—had become involved. He should have been in bed, but had instead come to the third storey. She wondered, too, why Mr. Mason quietly followed Mr. Rochester's orders and why Mr. Rochester had made sure that both of them remained quiet and secreted away. Jane remembered how Mr. Rochester had looked when he discovered Mr. Mason had arrived at the house, and feared what his coming to the house meant. Jane wondered when Mr. Rochester would return for them, particularly as Mr. Mason had turned quite pale and weak. Finally Mr. Rochester returned with a doctor and told him to work quickly. He wanted Mr. Mason to be back downstairs in half an hour. He asked Mr. Mason how he was. Mr. Mason, a chronic worrier, thought that he had been killed by her, but Mr. Rochester assured him he was fine. The doctor saw that the cut had been made with teeth. Mr. Mason admitted that he had been bitten after Mr. Rochester took the knife from her. He did not know what he should have done, especially as the woman was quiet when he first stepped in. Mr. Rochester told him it was his own fault for not waiting until the next day—they should have gone in together. Mr. Mason thought he might have done some good, but now he was suffering for not heeding Mr. Rochester's advice. Mr. Rochester told the doctor to hurry as the sun was rising. He wanted Mr. Mason gone. The doctor had finished with one set of wounds, but there were more bite marks in the other arm. Mr. Mason admitted she had sucked on his arm and sworn to drain his heart. Mr. Rochester told him not to repeat her words. Mr. Mason wished he could forget them. Mr. Rochester then told Jane to go to his room and fetch him a clean shirt.

When she returned, Mr. Rochester asked if anyone else was up. She assured him no one was awake. He sent Jane on a few more errands: once to retrieve Mr. Mason's fur lined cloak and then to fetch a small phial. It was a little bit of medicine Mr. Rochester had picked up in Italy. Mr. Mason did not want to drink it at first, but did so under Mr. Rochester's orders to do so. After a few minutes, he stood up and declared he felt a little better. Mr. Rochester sent Jane ahead of them to unlock the side door and tell the driver of the carriage to be ready for them. As she stood outside, she listened to the silence of the early morning. Mr. Rochester and the doctor helped Mr. Mason into the carriage. The doctor got in behind him and Mr. Rochester asked him to take care of his friend. Just as Mr. Rochester said his goodbyes, Mr. Mason asked that she be taken care of. Mr. Rochester assured him he did and would continue to do so, but as the carriage left he wished that there was an end to all of these problems. As Mr. Rochester walked toward a door in a wall around the orchard, Jane guessed that he was done with her and turned back toward the house. Mr. Rochester asked her to stay for a while in the fresh air, outside of the house that felt like a dungeon to him. The countryside, to him, was all that was real and pure. They walked through the orchard together as the sun rose.

Mr. Rochester offered her a flower and they discussed the sunrise for a moment. Jane asked if Grace Poole would be kept in the house. Mr. Rochester told her not to worry about that, but Jane feared for his safety while she stayed. Mr. Rochester could not assure her that his life would not be in danger from then on—he lived on the edge of it. Jane did not think Mr. Mason would harm or defy him, and Mr. Rochester agreed, but added he might ruin Mr. Rochester's happiness by accident. She advised him to let Mr. Mason know that he had to be careful and to show him how to avoid putting Mr. Rochester in further danger. Mr. Rochester admitted that he had always been able to tell Mr. Mason what to do, but he could not order him not to harm him. If he did that, he would have to reveal to Mr. Mason what *would* harm him, giving him power. He explained that Jane was his friend, but he would not be able to tell her his vulnerabilities just in case it gave her more power over him.

Mr. Rochester sat down on a bench and left room for Jane but she did not sit down. He wondered why she hesitated to sit. She sat, feeling that if she told him the reason for her hesitation, it would cause more trouble. Mr. Rochester asked her to imagine that she was a wild boy brought up in a foreign land and given all that he wanted. He asked her to imagine then that she had made a series of errors she could never put right and followed her throughout her life, even if she took steps to try and right the wrong. She would remain miserable and hope will have left her. He asks her to imagine that she has returned home after a long time away and made a new friend with the characteristics of someone she had looked for over twenty years. She would feel better around this person and a desire to carry on with life comes out of this friendship. Mr. Rochester asked her if this person would be able to overcome custom and dare to take an action that might cost him the opinion of those around him if it meant that he could be at peace. Jane answered that the salvation of a soul could only rely on God, and that this person should look to him for guidance. Mr. Rochester reveals that the person's case he was talking about was his own, and that he may have found the cure to his restless life in something. He paused for a moment, and then spoke again with a changed tone — more sarcastic and less gentle. He asked her if she thought his marriage to Miss Ingram might regenerate him, and then stood up without waiting for an answer. He returned a moment later and commented that Jane was quite pale. He wondered if she would curse him for keeping her up. Jane would not. He asked when she might sit up with him again, and she replied that she would whenever he needed her to. He suggested that she might sit with him the night before he was married about his lovely one. They were interrupted by the arrival of servants in the stables. Mr. Rochester sent her one way while he went the other to talk to the servants.

Chapter Twenty-One:

Jane remembered when she was six years old and overheard Bessie admit to another servant that she had dreamt about a small child, which was a sign of trouble to either herself or her family. Jane might have forgotten this statement had Bessie not had to return home the following day on account of her sister's death. Jane remembered this statement now because she had been dreaming of a child for seven nights straight. Jane did not like the recurrence of images, particularly this one, and she grew to dread bedtime. One day, Jane was called downstairs by the arrival of a man with a message for her. The man, a gentleman's servant, introduced himself as Leaven—he lived with Mrs. Reed at Gateshead as her coachman. He told her that John Reed had died in London after getting himself in debt and into jail twice. After he returned to Gateshead to demand his fortune and Mrs. Reed refused, John went back to London. The next they heard of him was that he died. There were rumours that he might have killed himself. Jane did not know what to say, but Leaven had more to say. Mrs. Reed had been quite sick and afraid that she might end up poor, and John's death was a shock to her system. She had a stroke and did not speak for three days. They could not work out what she was saying at first, but Bessie finally understood that she was repeating Jane's name and asking for her to be brought back to Gateshead. Bessie did not know if Mrs. Reed was losing her mind, so she asked the daughters who advised Bessie to send for Jane. Leaven wanted to take her back the next morning. Jane agreed that she should have to go. She sent Leaven to the servants' hall and went in search of Mr. Rochester to ask if she could go.

She found him with Miss Ingram, the Eshton daughters and their admiring gentleman in the billiard room playing a game. Jane tried to find her courage to interrupt the game as she could not avoid asking the question. As she approached Mr. Rochester, Miss Ingram turned to glare at her and looked tempted to order her away. Jane spoke his name, and Miss Ingram asked him if "that person" wanted him. Mr. Rochester grimaced and then followed Jane out of the room. Jane asked if she could leave for one or two weeks to see to Mrs. Reed. After questioning, Mr. Rochester discovers that Mrs. Reed was a relative despite Jane's earlier insistence that she had no relatives. Jane assured him that they did not consider one another family. Mr. Rochester had heard of John — he was considered a villain in London. He did not think that Jane could do any good by travelling a hundred miles to see her. She might even be dead before she reached Gateshead, and she did send Jane away. Jane argued that it was many years ago when she sent Jane away and it would not be easy to ignore a dying woman's wishes. Mr. Rochester asked her to promise to only stay for a week, but Jane could not keep that kind of promise. He agreed to let her go only on the condition that she return. Jane would if everything was well. He wanted to give her money to take with her, mentioning that he had not given her any salary yet. He took her purse from her and, seeing that she only had five shillings in it, gave her a fifty pound note. He only offered her fifteen and she had no change to give him. She did not want to take more than she was owed, so he took back the fifty and gave her ten. She pointed out that he still owed her five, but he wanted her to come back for it.

Jane mentioned Adele's future—if Mr. Rochester was to be married soon Adele would have to be sent away to school so she was not in Miss Ingram's way. Mr. Rochester agreed she should be sent away to school. He wondered if Jane would then go to the Devil. Jane hoped not—she would have to find another job elsewhere. Mr. Rochester wished he had not given her any money and asked her to hand it back to him. Jane refused. He asked her to promise not to advertise for a new governess position—he would help her find somewhere to go. Jane thanked him and reminded him that both she and Adele had to be out of the house before Miss Ingram moved in as his bride. Mr. Rochester promised. He wondered if he would see Jane again before she left, but Jane had to prepare for her journey. He asked how they would say goodbye, and Jane suggested that they just say farewell to one another for the time being. Mr. Rochester felt that they should do or say something else, but Jane was happy with the farewell and wondered when he might move away from the door so she could go and pack. When the dinner bell rang he disappeared without another word and Jane did not see him again before she left.

She arrived at Gateshead at five in the afternoon. She stepped into the lodge before she went to the main house to see the servants. Bessie sat on a chair nursing her newborn and the Leavens were pleased Jane had come. Jane hoped she was not too late. Mrs. Reed was still alive and still talking about her that morning. She was usually asleep for most of the afternoon, so they wondered if Jane would take a moment to rest. Jane agreed to do stay for a while and watched as Bessie moved around the house preparing tea. She would not let Jane come near the table and made her sit by the fireplace with her own little table. It reminded Jane of the old days. They talked about Thornfield, Mr. Rochester and the group of visitors who had been visiting the house. After an hour of gossip, Bessie helped Jane back into her bonnet and led her to the main house.

Jane remembered the morning Bessie had led her away from the house nine years previous. Jane had left the house with a bitter heart and she returned to it with more of an understanding of herself, even though her heart still ached. Her resentment toward the family had been lessened over time, too. Bessie sent her into the breakfast room, first, to sit with the Reed sisters. The room was exactly the same, but the ladies were very different. Eliza looked like a strict nun and Georgiana was a plump, pretty girl. They both stood and welcomed Jane with a polite "Miss Eyre". Eliza did not smile and immediately looked away, ignoring Jane, but Georgiana asked her general questions about the journey and so on. Jane could tell by Georgiana's glances that she did not approve of Jane's clothing or appearance, but her look did not affect her as much as it had in the past. Jane asked after Mrs. Reed. Georgiana did not think she would be able to see Jane that day, but Jane asked her to go up anyway and announce her arrival. She did not want to delay the visit any longer. Eliza told her that Mrs. Reed did not want to be disturbed in the evening. Jane told them that she would go and ask Bessie if Mrs. Reed wanted to see her that evening or not.

While Jane waited for Bessie to check in with Mrs. Reed, she reflected on change. In the past, Jane might have been tempted to leave Gateshead the following morning on account of the Reed sisters' cruelty towards her, but Jane knew better than that. She had to stay with Mrs. Reed until she was better or until she was dead and ignore the Reed sisters' proud attitude. She told the housekeeper she would probably be a visitor for one or two weeks and then met Bessie on the stairs. Bessie told her Mrs. Reed was awake. Jane stepped into the room which she had often visited to receive a telling off. She looked into the corner, half expecting to see the switch she had been hit with. Jane approached the bed and pulled the curtain back. She remembered that she had left Mrs. Reed with hate in her heart and had returned with a desire to forgive and to be reunited with her Aunt. She bent down and kissed her Aunt. She had vowed to never call her Aunt again, but she did not see sin in breaking that vow. She took Mrs. Reed's hand but, instead of squeezing her hand back, Mrs. Reed removed her hand and turned her face away. Jane knew that her attitude had not changed, and that she was determined to think she was bad until her dying day — to think otherwise would be to admit her treatment of Jane had been cruel. Jane felt pain, but then was determined to help her despite Mrs. Reed's attitude.

Jane told her she intended on staying. Mrs. Reed asked Jane if she had seen her daughters, and that she should tell them that she wanted Jane to stay until they could talk properly. She had things to tell Jane but could not quite remember what they were. Jane knew that the stroke had taken its toll on her Aunt. Mrs. Reed tried to pull the bed covers up around her, but Jane's elbow kept part of it down. She told Jane to move her arm and sit up, and then began discussing Jane as if Jane was not in the room. Mrs. Reed thought Jane had been a daily annoyance and burden to her. She had a temper and watched everyone constantly. She also talked to Mrs. Reed with anger like no other child seemed to have, and was glad to have sent her away to Lowood. She had hoped that Jane would have died from the fever because she had disliked her mother. Mrs. Reed's husband had loved Jane's mother, his sister, so much that he had cried for her when she died and sent for Jane to live with them. Mrs. Reed hated Jane the first moment she saw her, but Mr. Reed looked after Jane more than his own children. When he tried to make his children be kind to Jane and they refused, he grew angry with them. He made her promise to take care of Jane, or she would have sent the brat to a workhouse. She thought her husband was weak, and was glad that her son, John, was not like his father at all. She wished he would stop sending her letters asking for money. Jane thought it was best that she leave Mrs. Reed to rest. Bessie agreed — Mrs. Reed often talked this way in the evening. Before Jane left, Mrs. Reed told her to stop: she had another thing to say. She told Jane that he would constantly threaten to kill himself or her, but she did not know what to do or where to find the money. Bessie gave her a sedative and Mrs. Reed fell into a sleep.

Ten days went by before Jane had another conversation with her. Mrs. Reed was either delirious or extremely tired and the doctor forbid any activity that might have excited her. Jane tried to get on with her cousins as best she could. While Eliza ignored her and Georgiana talked endlessly to herself, Jane practised sketching. One day she started to draw a face, but did not know whose it was, and did not care to. Soon it took shape and Jane saw it was Mr. Rochester's face. Eliza had stepped up behind her and asked if she knew the person. Jane lied, telling her it was from her imagination, and put the sketch away. The drawings pleased both of the sisters, but Georgiana thought the image of Mr. Rochester was an ugly one. They were surprised by Jane's talent and asked her to draw them. Jane promised to contribute a water colour to Georgiana's album, which put her in a good mood. They went for a walk in the grounds together and Georgiana told her about her winter in London two years before. She made hints regarding the man she had attracted which grew as the day went on. Every day Georgiana talked about the same things, but strangely did not talk about her mother's illness or her brother's death, or even the family's probable poverty. She only spent five minutes with her mother a day. Eliza did not talk, nor did she seem to have time to talk. Jane did not know why she spent the day the way she did, with hours spent on prayer, sewing, gardening and on her accounts. Jane thought she was happy and nothing annoyed her to change her schedule in any way.

One evening Jane found her more willing to talk about her future. Eliza had made sure she had set money aside for herself, and when her mother died, whether or not she lived for a little longer or not, she would retire where she would not be disturbed by anyone else. Jane asked if Georgiana would go with her. She would not as Georgiana and Eliza had never had anything in common—they would each take their own course. Georgiana spent most of her days wishing that her Aunt would invite her to London again so that she could be out of the house until everything was over. Jane assumed that "everything" referred to the impending death of her mother. Eliza generally did not take any notice of her sister's complaints until one day when she set aside her projects and told her she was a vain creature who had no right to be born because she did not do anything with her life. She wondered if Georgiana had ever considered searching for her own independence and spending her days at work. If she did this, she would not have to rely on others for purpose in life. She will have found it for herself. Eliza told her after their mother's death she would wash her hands of Georgiana and they would have nothing to do with one another. Even if they were the only two people in the world, Eliza would still not have anything to do with her sister. Georgiana replied: she accused Eliza of being the most selfish, heartless person alive. Eliza could not bear her sister having a title higher than her own, which is why she ruined Georgiana's prospects. Jane considered that both of the girls suffered either from too much judgement without feeling, or too much feeling without judgement.

On a wet, windy afternoon while Eliza was at Church and Georgiana was asleep, Jane decided to go upstairs and see how Mrs. Reed was. No one really paid much attention to her—even Bessie had her own family to look after—so Jane found the room empty aside from Mrs. Reed. She tidied the room, and then stood at the window to watch the rain. She thought about Mrs. Reed whose spirit would leave them soon, and then remembered Helen Burns and her faith in the equality of souls. A weak voice cried out to Jane to ask who it was. Jane knew that Mrs. Reed had not spoken in days and thought she might be getting better. She went to her side and told her it was Jane. Mrs. Reed did not think it was Jane because she looked nothing like her, but Jane assured her she was Jane and explained how she had arrived from Thornfield. Mrs. Reed admitted that she was quite ill. She had been trying to move earlier but found she could not. She thought it was best that she ease her mind before she died so that she would not be burdened by regret.

After Mrs. Reed asked if they were alone and Jane assured her they were, Mrs. Reed admitted she had wronged her twice and regretted it. She broke her promise to her husband to protect Jane and bring her up as her own child. She hesitated at her second confession and wondered what would happen if she got better. It was painful for her to admit she was wrong. After a moment, Mrs. Reed decided that she had to get it over with as eternity was waiting for her. She told Jane to go to her dressing table and to take out the letter she saw there. Jane did. Mrs. Reed told her to read it aloud. The letter was from John Eyre, Jane's Uncle, asking for her address so that he could adopt her and leave her his fortune on his death. The letter was dated three years ago. Jane wondered why she never heard from him. Mrs. Reed admitted that it was because she hated Jane and did not want to help her toward a fortune. She never forgot the way Jane had told her she was the worst person in the world and accused her of being cruel. Jane told her not to think about her words anymore as she was a child when she spoke them. Mrs. Reed took her revenge by writing to John Eyre and telling him Jane had died of fever at Lowood. She told Jane she could write to him and expose her lies if she wanted, but either way she thought Jane had been born to be her tormenter; she would have never been tempted to do this to anyone else but Jane. Jane asked her to forget their past and treat her with kindness. She was not vindictive, but passionate as a child, and she would have done anything to make Mrs. Reed love her. She asked Mrs. Reed to kiss her, but she only pulled away and demanded some water. Jane took her hand, but she pulled her hand away. Jane told her she could love or hate her as she would still have her forgiveness either way.

The nurse and Bessie stepped into the room, and Jane stayed for half an hour to see if Mrs. Reed changed her mind, but she did not. She died that night at midnight. Neither she or any of her daughters were there to close her eyes. Eliza and Jane went to look at her, but Georgiana could not go. Jane felt sorry for her. Eliza announced that her mother should have lived far longer if she had not been troubled, gave a faint hint at emotion and then left the room. Neither of them cried.

Chapter Twenty Two:

Mr. Rochester had only given Jane a week's absence from Thornfield, but she had spent an entire month at Gateshead before leaving. Jane wanted to leave just after the funeral, but Georgiana had made her promise to stay until she left for London, where she had finally been invited to. Georgiana did not want to be left alone with Eliza, who did not sympathize with her or help her with her preparations. Jane dealt with Georgiana's selfishness, did her sewing for her and helped to pack her dresses while Georgiana sat by and watched. If she and Jane were going to spend more time together, Jane would not have let her get away with it and would have forced her to do her own work. As their time together would be short, however, she decided to be patient. When Georgiana left, Eliza asked Jane to stay for another week. Her plans required all of her time and she spent every day locked in her room, filling her trunks, burning papers and refusing to talk to anyone else. She wanted Jane to look after the house and answer letters. One morning, Eliza told Jane she could leave when she wanted and thanked her for her help. She thought Jane was better than Georgiana as she played her part in life without burdening anyone. She would leave for a nunnery in Europe the following day so she could spend her time quietly in study of Roman Catholic dogma. Jane thought it would be a good fit for her. They wished one another well and parted company. Georgiana eventually married a wealthy man, and Eliza spent her days in the convent.

Jane had never experienced pleasure associated with returning home—she never knew what to expect when she returned to Gateshead, or to Lowood. She had never experienced returning home to Thornfield and wondered what it might be like. Her journey back was tedious and she thought of Mrs. Reed in her last moments and the funeral, and then of the two Reed sisters. She wondered how long she would stay at Thornfield. She didn't think it would be long at all. She had heard from Mrs. Fairfax that Mr. Rochester had gone to London three weeks before, and that he would be expected back in two weeks. She had told Jane that he had gone to make arrangements for his wedding to Miss Ingram, even though she thought it was an odd match. Everyone Mrs. Fairfax spoke to about it seemed sure that the event would take place very soon. Jane dreamed of Miss Ingram that night. She closed the gates to Thornfield and pointed to the road. Mr. Rochester stood there with his arms folded and staring at them both. Jane had not told Mrs. Fairfax that she was returning as she did not want to be met at Millcote. She wanted to walk from Millcote to Thornfield by herself. Jane felt joy as she walked, and she wondered what it meant, especially as Thornfield was not a permanent home to her. She would have to leave soon. Mrs. Fairfax and Adele would be happy to see her, but Jane knew she was thinking of Mr. Rochester, and that he was not thinking of her. She did not mind, however, and only wanted the privilege of looking at him, even if he ignored her. She could be close to him while she could, but after he was married they would be separated for forever. She made an agonized sound and then ran toward Thornfield.

Although the countryside was beautiful, Jane did not want to stay to look around her. She came to the stile she once sat on and found Mr. Rochester there with book and pencil in his hand, writing. Jane is unable to move for a moment. She did not know why he was sat there and wanted to ask him, but almost didn't trust her own voice. She did not want to make a fool of herself and wondered for a moment if she could slip away and take a different route to the house. However, Mr. Rochester spotted her and told her to come along. He told her that it was one of her tricks not to let them know she was coming and to not send for a carriage. He asked her what she had been doing for the past month. Jane replied that she had been with her aunt, who had died. Mr. Rochester suggested she was a spirit from another world, and wondered if she was an elf. Jane knew that he would not be her master for too much longer, but his ability to make her happy and to suggest it was important to him if she thought about him or not was an addictive feeling. They discussed his errand to London to buy a carriage for Miss Ingram, who would soon be Mrs. Rochester. He wished that he was a more handsome man. If she was a fairy, he wondered if she could transform him. Jane suggested that to anyone who loved him he was a beautiful man. He smiled at her with a smile he only used on rare occasions. Jane went over the stile and meant to leave him calmly, but a force stronger than her turned her around and thanked Mr. Rochester for his kindness. She told him that she was happy to be with him again, and that home for her was wherever he is. She walked quickly away from him: so fast that he could not have caught her.

Everyone at Thornfield greeted her with warm enthusiasm. Jane thought it was pleasant being loved by others and feeling that there were people who wanted her around. She closed her mind to the thought that she would one day have to leave Thornfield, and uttered a silent prayer that she would not have to leave for a far away place or for long. She sat with the others enjoying a quiet night. Mr. Rochester stepped in and seemed to be satisfied by what he saw in the peaceful gathering. Jane hoped that he would keep them altogether even after the marriage so that they would not have to leave his presence.

A fortnight passed. Nothing more was said or done as preparation for the marriage, and Jane asked Mrs. Fairfax every day if anything had been decided. Her answer was always no. One day Mrs. Fairfax asked Mr. Rochester when he was going to bring his bride home, but he only answered with a joke and a queer look on his face. She did not know what he meant by that. The other thing that surprised Jane was that there were no visits to Ingram Park. It was twenty miles away, but Jane did not think that distances would keep lovers away from one another. Mr. Rochester was a great horseman and it would have only taken him a morning to ride it. Jane started to hope that the match between him and Miss Ingram had been broken, and that the rumours had been mistaken ones. She tried to see if Mr. Rochester was upset or angry, but she could not remember a time when he had not been so happy. He called Jane into his presence more often than ever and was always kind to her. Jane had never loved him more.

Chapter Twenty Three:

The Midsummer weather was beautiful. Adele, tired after gathering wild strawberries for half a day, had gone to bed as soon as the sun set. Jane went back out into the garden to enjoy what she thought was the sweetest hour of the day: just after sunset. Jane smelled cigar smoke and saw the library window open slightly, so she went into the orchard so she wouldn't be watched while she took her walk. As she enjoyed the countryside, she smelled Mr. Rochester's cigar smoke again, and knew that he was close by. Jane turned to see him stepping into the orchard. Jane sat in a small hiding spot, hoping that he would leave again soon. He did not. He stopped to smell the flowers and look around him. When a moth landed on a plant near his foot, he stooped to examine it. Jane thought she could sneak away while he had his back to her. As she passed behind him, he told her to come and see the moth. She did not know how he knew she was there, but still came to see it.

Mr. Rochester thought it reminded him of a West Indies insect. Just after the moth flew away, Jane moved back toward the house, but Mr. Rochester followed her, wondering why she wanted to go back into the house on such a nice night. Jane could not think of an excuse: she did not want to walk around in the orchard by herself with Mr. Rochester, but did not know what she could say without being impolite or revealing how she really felt. Even though she walked with him, she only thought about ways she might be able to escape. They talked about Thornfield. Mr. Rochester suggested that she must have become quite attached to the house, but did not know why she cared so much for Adele or Mrs. Fairfax. He asked if she would be upset if she had to leave them. She admitted she would be. Mr. Rochester thought that was a pity—it was normal for people to have to leave places they had found themselves comfortable in. Jane asked if she had to leave Thornfield. Mr. Rochester agreed that she had. Jane knew then that he would be married to Miss Ingram and Mr. Rochester confirmed it. He reminded her that it was Jane's idea that Adele and Jane would have to leave once the marriage was over with. Jane agreed to find somewhere else to work. Mr. Rochester offered to help her find a new position in the next month. Lady Ingram had already found a suitable place for her with the O'Galls in Ireland teaching their five daughters, but Jane did not want to go as far as Ireland if it meant being so far away from Mr. Rochester.

It was an announcement that she had not meant to make, and she burst into tears. The thought of a sea between her and Mr. Rochester upset her a great deal. Mr. Rochester suggested that friends who had been close to one another often found themselves upset at a separation, and that they should spend as much time together as possible before it happened. He was sorry that she would have to go so far away and would try to find something better for her, but could not promise he would be able to. Mr. Rochester wondered if Jane felt something different for him. He admitted that he sometimes had a strange feeling when he was close to her. He did not know if the separation would lead him to bleeding internally. He was sure that she would forget him, though. Jane assured him she would never forget him. Mr. Rochester told her to listen to the nightingale, which she did, but sobbed at the same time. She wished she had never been born or ever come to Thornfield. Mr Rochester wondered why. Jane admitted she loved Thornfield — she had not been scared or treated cruelly and as an inferior. The prospect of being separated from Mr. Rochester terrified her but it was necessary. Mr. Rochester was confused at first by what she meant and suggested he had no bride in Miss Ingram, and then ground his teeth. Jane knew she had to go. Mr. Rochester did not want her to. Jane stood and asked him if she was meant to deal with being nothing to him. She was not a machine without feelings. She had a heart and a soul, and if she had wealth and beauty it would have been hard for him to refuse her. She knew she was not talking to him with the traditional class custom, but she did not care: they were talking to one another as people. Mr. Rochester pulled Jane into his arms and kissed her. Jane reminded him he was about to be a married man, even to someone inferior to him and to someone he did not love. He had to let her go to Ireland. Mr. Rochester would not let her go. Jane asked him to let her go as she was a free person and wanted to leave him. Mr. Rochester told her she should decide her own destiny: he offered her his hand in marriage and his love. Jane told him not to make jokes. Mr. Rochester assured her he wanted to marry her. They sat quietly. Jane cried.

After a moment he suggested they should try to understand one another. He only wanted to marry her. Jane kept quiet, believing that he was making fun of her. Mr. Rochester again stated he wanted to marry her — his equal — and wanted her for his wife. He asked if she doubted him. She did. He tried to explain: he had no love for Miss Ingram, and she had none for him. He made sure she heard a rumour that her fortune was a third of what she thought it was, and afterwards noticed how cold she and her mother became. He could not marry someone like that. Jane did not understand why he would marry someone so poor and unconnected. Mr. Rochester insisted that he wanted her for his own. Jane looked at his face — he was flushed and emotional. He claimed she was torturing him. Jane could not torture him. If his feelings were real, she would only be grateful. He begged her to accept him and to use his first name, Edward. After he assured her he truly loved her, Jane accepted Mr. Rochester and they were engaged. After holding one another for a moment, Mr. Rochester begged that God would not allow anyone else to come between them. Mr. Rochester talked to himself — he hoped that God would understand that "she" had been cold to him, and that he would guard and love Jane. He did not care about the world judging him.

Suddenly a storm erupted, and Mr. Rochester rushed Jane through the gardens to the house. They were very wet when they finally made it into the hall, and Mr. Rochester helped her with her shawl. Mrs. Fairfax stepped out into the hall, although Jane and Mr. Rochester did not see her. Mr. Rochester told Jane to go and change, and wished his darling a good night. He kissed her repeatedly. When Jane left his arms, she noticed the pale looking Mrs. Fairfax watching them. She smiled, did not explain, and went up the stairs. Jane would explain another day. Although the storm raged outside her window, Jane was overjoyed and not afraid. Mr. Rochester came to her door three times to see if she was alright, and this gave her strength.

The next morning, Adele ran into her bedroom to tell her that the giant chestnut tree at the bottom of the orchard had been struck by lightning and split down the middle.

Chapter Twenty-Four:

As Jane got ready for the day, she thought about what had happened the day before and considered that it might have been a dream. She could not be certain it had happened until she saw Mr. Rochester again and heard his words of love for her. Jane looked at herself in the mirror and did not think she was plain anymore. She had often avoided looking at Mr. Rochester in case he thought she was average looking, but she was sure she could look at him now. She ran down the hall and was pleased that there was a beautiful June morning waiting for her. It seemed that nature was happy for her, too. Jane saw a beggar woman and her son walking up the path and ran to give them all the money she had in her purse.

Mrs. Fairfax asked her to come into breakfast with a sad look on her face. She did not speak much, but Jane could not explain what had happened yet. That was up to Mr. Rochester. Jane hurried upstairs to Adele, but passed her on the way to the schoolroom. Adele had been sent to the nursery. Jane found Mr. Rochester in one of the bedrooms. He greeted her with a hug and kiss, which seemed natural to Jane. He reminded her that she would soon be Jane Rochester — within four weeks! It made Jane feel giddy just thinking about it. She was happy but afraid. Most people would never find themselves completely happy, and for Jane to think that she might be would be a lie. Mr. Rochester disagreed — he would make her happy. He had written to his banker that morning to ask for the jewels he had in storage to be sent to Thornfield for Jane to wear. Jane did not want jewels — it would be strange for her to have them. Mr. Rochester wanted to place jewels on her wrists, fingers and around her neck. Jane insisted that she wanted to be treated like the person she was, and not like nobility or like a beautiful woman. Mr. Rochester insisted that she was beautiful to him. Jane thought he must be dreaming, then. Mr. Rochester ignored her and declared that he would make sure the rest of the world knew she was beautiful as well. Jane argued that she wouldn't be Jane Eyre anymore if he did that. He would be turning her into something different. She didn't want him to compliment her. Mr. Rochester ignored her. He wanted to take her into Millcote so that they could buy some dresses for her to wear.

The marriage would take place in the Church close by and then they would go to London, France and Italy. Jane would learn to value herself when she saw how other people lived. Mr. Rochester once travelled through Europe full of bitterness and hate, and now he would return to the same places as if healed and with an angel as his companion. Jane laughed: she was not an angel, and he should not think of herself as one. She only wanted to be herself. They discuss their expectations for the future: Jane thinks that Mr. Rochester might end up falling out of love with her in six months, and will only grow to like her again but never love her. She had read many books by men that suggest this period of time is the most that any husband will love his wife. Mr. Rochester denies this — he will only love her more. He had never met anyone like her and would only love her for forever. Jane still wonders how he will think of her in a year from now. She asks him not to send for golds or jewels. Mr. Rochester agrees not to do so but still wants to give her a present.

Jane wants to ask questions, but Mr. Rochester will not answer questions about secrets. He would rather give her half his fortune. Jane doesn't know what she would do with half his estate. He will open up to her, but does not want to burden her with troubling thoughts. She argues with him: he had suggested mere moments before that he liked to be conquered by her, but now he backed away. Jane suggested she should persuade him to confess his secrets and cry if he needed more incentive. Mr. Rochester didn't think she would dare. Jane pointed to his stern face — this would be the way he looked at her after they were married. Mr. Rochester told her to ask her question. Before Jane did she told him she preferred being treated rudely than like an angel. She asked him why he went to so much trouble to convince her he was marrying Miss Ingram. Mr. Rochester was happy that this was the question and lost his troubled look. Mr. Rochester wanted to make Jane as jealous of Miss Ingram as possible so he could secure her hand in marriage. Jane told him his behaviour was disgraceful. She wondered if he thought about Miss Ingram's feelings at all, but he argued she needed a little humbling. Jane wanted to know if Miss Ingram was suffering at all. Mr. Rochester assured her she wasn't. Jane asked Mr. Rochester to tell Mrs. Fairfax about their engagement to ease her shock. She did not want to be misjudged by her friend. Mr. Rochester told her to get ready for their trip to Millcote while he did.

When Jane was ready and Mr. Rochester had left Mrs. Fairfax's room, Jane rushed into it. Mrs. Fairfax stared at the wall, lost in thought. When she saw Jane she tried to smile and congratulate her, but could not finish the sentence. She wondered if she was dreaming and asked Jane to confirm that she was marrying Mr. Rochester. Jane confirmed it. Mrs. Fairfax could not believe someone as proud as Mr. Rochester would marry someone poor. She did not know how it was possible and suggested that marriage between classes and great differences in ages did not end well. Mrs. Fairfax asked if they were really marrying for love. Jane was hurt by her questions that she almost started to cry. Mrs. Fairfax apologized for treating her coldly but wanted Jane to be careful. She thought both of them would discover new things about one another that might shock them. Mrs. Fairfax hoped that everything would work out in the end and advised Jane to be careful, to keep Mr. Rochester at a distance and distrust both her feelings and his. Gentlemen did not marry their governesses. Thankfully for Jane, Adele ran in asking to accompany them to Millcote. Jane took Adele outside where Mr. Rochester was waiting for the carriage. Jane asked for Adele to come with them, but Mr. Rochester thought she would only get in the way. When he noticed how upset Jane looked, he wondered if it would make her sad not to have Adele with her, and then allowed her to come with them. During the ride, Mr. Rochester told Adele that the image of Jane had appeared to him and gave him a gold ring. To him, Jane was a fairy. Jane told Adele not to listen to him.

Their trip to Millcote was a stressful one for Jane. Mr. Rochester wanted Jane to order half a dozen dresses, but she did not want to. She managed to persuade him to only buy two dresses, but he wanted to choose these two for himself. Jane nervously watched him as he looked around the store and picked two brightly coloured dresses. If he bought them, Jane would refuse to wear them, and suggested he should buy black and grey. He agreed but declared he would see her in brighter clothing in the future. Mr. Rochester then took them to a jewellers and embarrassed Jane with the amount he bought for her.

When they returned to Thornfield in the carriage, Jane remembered the letter from her Uncle. She would write to him as soon as they got back to the house as it would be a relief to have some financial independence. After she wrote the letter, Jane could once again meet Mr. Rochester's eye. She found him looking at her like a master after he had given presents to his slave and told him not to look at her like that. If he did, she would only wear her Lowood dresses. Mr. Rochester celebrated her originality. He would not trade her for any other girl. After a brief discussion of slavery, Mr. Rochester wanted Jane to give up her governess position at once. Jane refused. She wanted things to continue the way they had been: she would teach during the day, and he would call for her if he required her presence. Mr. Rochester reluctantly agreed but warned her that she would not be able to get away from him once they were married.

He called for her that night, but Jane had a plan. She tricked him into playing the piano for them while she sat looking out of the window. It was a love song, and Mr. Rochester stood up after he finished with a face full of passion. Jane did not want this sort of behaviour — it frightened her. She asked him what he meant when he sang about a wife dying with her husband. Jane would rather die in her own time. He wondered if she would forgive him for his selfish idea with a kiss, but Jane would have rather gone to her room. Now irritated, Mr. Rochester went to the other side of the room. Jane stood up, respectfully said good-night and left the room. She continued on in this way. Mr. Rochester was generally angry, but Jane could see that he was entertained by it. If Jane had been more submissive, he would have been endlessly bored by it. When she was around other people she continued to be quiet, but when she and Mr. Rochester were alone she wound him up. Instead of compliments, he called her a puppet and changeling, and instead of caresses, he pinched her. She preferred this than tender treatment, and so did Mrs. Fairfax. Jane did not find this an easy task as she would have rather pleased Mr. Rochester. He was becoming her whole world, and even overtaking her thoughts of God, Heaven and religion.

Chapter Twenty-Five:

The month had almost passed, and the preparations for the wedding had been completed. Jane had nothing left to do: her trunks were packed, and tomorrow they would be on their way to London. Jane would no longer be Jane Eyre, but Jane Rochester. Mr. Rochester had written this name on several cards to label the trunks, but Jane could not bring herself to have them stuck to the trunks. Jane Rochester did not exist and would not exist until the next day. Even her wardrobe was alien to her — her Lowood frocks had been replaced with shimmery, white dresses. Jane was anxious, but the wedding the next day was not the only thing that was making her so. Mr. Rochester had gone missing. He had left for a few farms her owned and had not returned that night yet.

Jane went out into the orchard and walked toward the split chestnut tree. Jane was sure there was still life in the tree even if there would be no more leaves. At last each part of the tree had the other and still clung together. The wind dropped for a moment to give way for a wail. Jane could not figure out where it had come from, so she ran again. She wandered back into the house, tidied up the library and was still restless. She did not want to stay in the house, so ran down to the gates to see if Mr. Rochester was coming. Jane saw no Mr. Rochester. She began to cry and even the moon disappeared behind the clouds. She was worried he had been involved in an accident. She remembered what had happened the previous night and wondered if it had been an omen. She could not sit in the house waiting for him — she would rather keep walking toward him. She walked quickly. Finally a horseman came her way, and it was Mr. Rochester. He knew she couldn't do without him, and pulled her onto the horse in front of him. Although he was pleased she wanted to see him so much, he asked what might have happened. Jane admitted she was worried he wouldn't come. There was something else that was troubling her but she did not want to tell him about it just yet. Mr. Rochester was as worried as he had been all month — Jane had been a tricky thing the entire month and he wasn't sure they would actually be married, and *now* she was needy.

When they arrived at Thornfield, Mr. Rochester made Jane promise to change her rain soaked clothes quickly and return to the library. She did, and found him eating. He asked her to join him as it would be one of the last meals they would have at Thornfield for a while. Jane couldn't eat—everything else in her life seemed surreal. Even Mr. Rochester was like a dream to him—she could touch him, but that was part of the dream. When he finished eating, Jane sat near Mr. Rochester. He reminded her of her promise to stay up with him the night before his wedding. Jane couldn't sleep anyway—she didn't want to go to bed. Mr. Rochester told her that they would leave Thornfield half an hour after their return from Church. He wondered why her cheeks were red and her eyes glittered—he asked if she was feeling well. Jane thought she was. Mr. Rochester wondered what she meant by that and asked her to describe how she felt. Jane didn't know how she felt, and she did not know what the future held for her. She did not feel calm, but she was happy. Mr. Rochester asked her to tell him if something was wrong—if she was afraid he would not be a good husband for her. Jane thought he would be a good husband. He wondered if she was afraid of hew new life. She was not. He was not convinced that she was feeling well, however, and pushed for an explanation. Jane told him that something had happened the previous day. She had been extremely busy all day getting ready and was not afraid of what the future would bring. She spent most of the day thinking about Mr. Rochester and wondering what kind of life they would have together. At sunset, the air turned cold. Sophie called Jane upstairs to look at her wedding dress which had just arrived. She found the veil which Mr. Rochester had bought as a present, too. Jane had smiled when she'd seen it, thinking that this was the way he was getting back at her for refusing jewels. Jane planned on wearing a handkerchief on her head and teasing him about the veil, and imagined what Mr. Rochester might have said to her when she did. The veil itself did not scare her. It signified pride, but she was used to it. The wind blew and it sounded like someone moaning. It worried Jane so much that she couldn't sleep for a long time.

When she did sleep, she had a dream about being separated from Mr. Rochester. There was a small child Jane held in her arms which cried endlessly. She knew Mr. Rochester was on the road ahead of her, and she tried her best to find him or stop him from moving, but nothing she did stopped him. Mr. Rochester told her not to be unhappy—they were close together and would not be separated. Jane wanted to tell him the rest of the story, and Mr. Rochester was surprised to hear there was more to tell. Jane had another dream that Thornfield Hall was in ruins. She wandered across the grounds still carrying the little child. She did not want to continue carrying it, but could not place it down anywhere. She heard a horse galloping in the road and was sure that it was Mr. Rochester. She thought he was going away and leaving for a distant country. She climbed a wall to watch him go when a rock gave way under her hands and the child clung to her neck, almost strangling her. Jane finally made it to the top of the wind, but she could not stand up. Mr. Rochester disappeared into the distance. The wall crumbled underneath her, the child rolled away and Jane fell. Mr. Rochester was certain that this was the end of the story. Jane told him there was more.

When she woke, she thought that it was the morning as a bright light shone in her room. It was actually someone with a candle. Jane thought it was Sophie, and asked her what she was doing rummaging in her closet. The figure turned and it was not Sophie, Leah, Mrs. Fairfax or Grace Poole. Mr. Rochester argued that it had to be one of them. Jane swore that the figure was a stranger to her. It was a woman with thick, dark hair wearing white. She did not see the figure's face at first, but when she picked up Jane's veil and placed it over her own head, Jane saw the reflection of her face in the mirror. She described the face as a ghastly, savage face. The woman tore the veil in half and stamped on it. She then pulled the curtains, looked outside, and then took the candle and went to leave the room. Just before she left, she held the candle in front of Jane's face and blew it out. Jane fainted. When she woke up, it was daytime and decided not to tell anyone but Mr. Rochester about the woman she had seen. She demanded he tell her who it was. Mr. Rochester thought her nerves had made her imagine the woman. Jane knew that it had happened—even if Thornfield was not in ruins, and Mr. Rochester had not left her yet, her veil had been found torn in two. Mr. Rochester embraced her, pleased that she had not been hurt. He provided an explanation: Grace Poole must have entered her room in the middle of the night in a delirious state. He asked if she had ever wondered why Grace had been kept in the house, especially after what she did to Mason. Everything that happened to Jane in her room was real, and it was done by Grace, but he would not tell her why he kept her in the house until they had been married for a year and a day. Jane decided it was the only possible explanation even though she was not satisfied by it, and made an effort to appear relieved.

Just as they went up to bed, Mr. Rochester told Jane she should sleep in Adele's bed with her that night to avoid anymore nightmares. She had to make sure the door was securely locked as well. He predicted that she would sleep soundly and dream of happy things that night, but Jane did not sleep at all. She watched Adele, a picture of childhood innocence and passion, and waited for her wedding day to come. Adele clung to her in the morning, and Jane tried not to cry as they left one another just in case she upset the little girl. Adele was a symbol of her past life, and now she must meet her future.

Chapter Twenty-Six:

Sophie came to help Jane dress for the wedding and took such a long time that Mr. Rochester asked why Jane had not come down. Jane hurried out of Sophie's hands as soon as she could, but Sophie told her to stop and look at herself in the mirror for a moment. Jane did and saw her strange reflection in the mirror looking back at her. When she finally made it down the stairs, Mr. Rochester told her she had taken too long and that they would not have long to eat dinner. While she ate, Mr. Rochester made sure that the carriage had been packed with their luggage and things. He wanted it ready to leave as soon as they returned from the Church. Mr. Rochester led her out into the hall and walked her past Mrs. Fairfax. Jane wanted to speak to her, but he had gripped her hand too hard and looked like he wouldn't be able to delay the wedding a second longer. Jane wondered if other bridegrooms looked like he did on his wedding day. He looked determined and grim as they made their way to the Church. Jane stared at him, wondering what made him look so fierce and think so hard. As they walked toward the gate on foot, Mr. Rochester discovered that Jane was out of breath and turned to ask her if she thought he was cruel in his love of her. He gave her a moment to rest and recover. She watched a couple reading gravestones who went inside the Church after a moment. When Jane was recovered, he led her inside the Church.

It was quiet in the Church and only two people — the couple from the graveyard — stood in the corner near the Rochester vault, their backs to them. As the ceremony began, one of the strangers — a gentleman — stepped toward them. After a while, the clergyman asked them both if they knew of any reason why they should not be married to one another. He paused, as custom expected, and began to continue when the stranger interrupted: he knew why the marriage could not take place. Silence descended on the Church, Jane and the clergyman looked round, but Mr. Rochester told him to continue the ceremony. The clergyman could not until they had investigated the claim. Mr. Rochester again ignored the stranger as he echoed his previous statement. The speaker told them that Mr. Rochester already had a living wife. The words this stranger spoke made Jane a little angry, but she did not swoon. She made Mr. Rochester look at her — he said nothing to her, and pulled her close. He asked who the stranger was. He was a solicitor from London and his name was Mr. Briggs. He wanted to remind Mr. Rochester of his living wife's existence, and removed a piece of paper from his pocket to read from. It stated that Mr. Rochester had married Bertha Antoinetta Mason in Spanish Town, Jamaica. Mr. Rochester argued that, even if the document was official, there was no proof that she was still alive. Mr. Briggs knew that she was living three months ago still and had a witness to prove it. He asked Mr. Mason to step forward. Mr. Rochester started to shake with fury or despair — Jane did not know which.

The other man was Mr. Mason, and Mr. Rochester raised his arm as if about to strike him. Mr. Mason pulled back, but Mr. Rochester calmed down and did not hit him. The clergyman asked Mr. Mason if the wife was still alive. Mr. Mason told them that he was her brother and that she was still living at Thornfield Hall in April when he had visited. The clergyman had never heard of a Mrs. Rochester at Thornfield. He thought it was impossible. Mr. Rochester muttered to himself that he had taken measures to make sure no one had heard about her or referred to her with that name. Mr. Rochester had aimed to marry Jane even though he was still married to Bertha Mason, and now his plan had failed. He admitted that the mysterious lunatic that lived in his house was his wife. He had sometimes told people she was his half-sister or mistress, but she was his wife of fifteen years. She was a mad woman and had come from a mad family. He discovered this after he married her, thought he was a happy man, and discovered her madness. Grace Poole looked after her in the house. Mr. Rochester assured them all that Jane had no idea Bertha even existed, and invited them all up to the house to see his mad wife.

Mr. Rochester dragged Jane out of the Church with the three gentlemen following. He sent the carriage away as they would not be needing it. Mrs. Fairfax, Adele and others had gathered to congratulate them, but he sent them away too. He led them up the stairs, still holding Jane's hand, and went straight to the third storey. They went into the room with the tapestry. He lifted the tapestry, reminding Mason that he was bitten by his sister here, and then opened the door. The room had no window and was lit by a fire. Grace Poole bent over the fire cooking in a saucepan. A figure ran around in the far end of the room on all fours. She was covered in thick, frizzed hair and clothes. When Mr. Rochester said hello to them, the figure stood and cried at them. Grace told them to be careful and leave, but Mr. Rochester wanted a moment with them. He did not think she had a knife on her, so she would not be too much of a danger to them. Grace argued that she was cunning, and told them to beware. Mr. Rochester pushed Jane behind him as his wife jumped towards them and grabbed his throat. They struggled: she was a strong woman and gave Mr. Rochester quite a fight. He could have struck her to end the fight, but only wrestled with her instead. When he finally had her under control, Grace gave him some rope and he tied her arms behind her. He then tied her to a chair. His wife yelled and tried to escape the chair. He turned to the guests and announced to them that she was his wife, and her attack was the only embrace he would receive from her. He asked them not to judge him for wanting to be rid of her and move on with his life, and then led them out of the room, waiting behind for a moment to talk to Grace.

Mr. Briggs told Jane that she would not be blamed for anything that had happened, and that her Uncle would be happy to hear it. Jane discovered that Mr. Mason knew her Uncle, who was unfortunately very sick and probably close to dying. After hearing about her difficult situation from Mr. Mason, he was upset that he could not rush to Jane's side to help her escape and asked Mr. Mason to rescue her. Mr. Briggs and he were grateful that they were not too late. If Mr. Briggs could be certain that her Uncle would still be alive once she travelled to Madeira, he would have suggested that she go to him, but he was sure she would be too late. It would be better for her to stay in England. The clergyman and Mr. Mason said goodbye to her, and then left. Jane withdrew to her own room, locked the door and very calmly took off her wedding dress. She sat down, suddenly weak, and began to think about what she'd seen. She was surprised that the encounter had been such a calm, quiet one. There had been hardly any tears and Mr. Rochester had provided explanations and evidence when asked. Nothing had really changed, but the Jane Eyre of yesterday had gone. She wondered where she had gone. She was now a cold, solitary person again. Her hopes were dead, her wishes gone, and her love for Mr. Rochester could never provide her warmth again. He had not betrayed her, but he had held the truth from her. She was sure he would not want to see her again as he would probably hate the sight of her. Jane was surprised how blind she had been to the truth. Jane had no strength left and she wished for death. There was only one thing inside her that gave her strength and power, and that was remembering God. She could not utter a single word, but prayed in her mind.

Chapter Twenty-Seven:

Jane finally sat up sometime in the afternoon of that day. She wondered what to do, and the answer that popped into her head — to leave Thornfield right away — was an awful thought. She was not Mr. Rochester's bride, but she could not leave him. Another voice told her that she should do it. She struggled with her thoughts. She stood up suddenly, weakened by hunger and thirst, and terrified by the silence of her room. She realized that she had had no visitors or messages at all to ask how she was. She opened the door and stumbled out, but an arm caught her. Jane looked up to find Mr. Rochester sat in a chair across from her bedroom door. He was glad she finally came out. He had heard no noises from her room and was almost starting to consider breaking down the door. He did not like that she grieved by herself. He would have rather her cause a scene of passion. He was prepared for and wanted tears, but he saw she had not cried at all. She did not reply. Mr. Rochester argued that he had not meant to hurt her, and wondered if she would ever forgive him. Jane did forgive him as he looked so unhappy. Mr. Rochester tested the waters by asking her if she thought he was a scoundrel. He might not have expected her to, but Jane agreed that he was a scoundrel. She was not weak willed. He did not want to be spared from her feelings, but Jane could not say anything. She was tired and needed some water. Mr. Rochester took her in his arms and carried her downstairs. He gave her wine and something to eat, and then Jane realized where he had brought her: the library. Jane considered that if she died right that moment, she would not have to suffer through being separated from Mr. Rochester. She did not want to leave him, and didn't think she could, but she knew she had to.

Mr. Rochester tried to kiss her, but Jane moved her head away from him. He already had a wife! He argued that she must think he plotted to strip her of her honour. He accused her of wanting to act against him. Jane did not. Mr. Rochester knew she was plotting to turn them into strangers again, and live in Thornfield just as Adele's governess. Jane disagreed — Adele should have a new governess to avoid conflict between them. Mr. Rochester has decided that Adele will go to school, and he did not intend on keeping Jane at Thornfield. It would only haunt her. He thought it was wrong for him to have brought her to the house knowing that Bertha Mason lived within it. He couldn't send her away elsewhere, even though he owned an old house called Ferndean Manor where she might have lived. He will nail the doors and windows to Thornfield shut and gave Grace money to live with Bertha. Jane stopped him, then, and told him he was too cruel to his wife as she could not help being mad. Mr. Rochester did not hate his wife because she was mad. If Jane was mad, he would still love her, no matter if she thought otherwise. Mr. Rochester returned to his earlier statement: Jane's belongings were already waiting for her in the carriage, so she would leave the very next day. Mr. Rochester would leave for another place, and Adele would be sent away to school — he did not care for his French mistress' bastard child. Jane worried about him being left by himself. Mr. Rochester did not understand what she meant by that — she would be going with him! Jane shook her head. Mr. Rochester wondered if she would listen to reason, and if not, if she might listen to violence. He looked like a man about to plunge into a passionate frenzy, but Jane was not afraid. She felt powerful. She knew the situation was a troubling one, but kept calm and took Mr. Rochester's hand. She would talk to him for as long as he wanted her to. Jane cried. Mr. Rochester told her to stop — he couldn't talk to her while she cried — but she couldn't while he was still angry. He insisted he wasn't angry. He just couldn't cope. He asked if she did not love him, and if she was only marrying him for his fortune and status. Jane did love him, but she could not show it. He wondered if she would be able to live with him and still repress her emotions, but Jane admitted she planned to leave him for good. She had to begin a new life. Mr. Rochester ignored what she said about leaving him — that was madness. She would begin a new life, but with him. They would travel to France and live a happy, innocent life together there. Jane had to be reasonable. Jane would not go with him — he had a living wife, and if Jane lived with him she would be his mistress, no matter what he said. Mr. Rochester warned her he was getting angry. Jane asked for God's help. Mr. Rochester just wanted her to listen to him: if he explained the circumstances he married his wife in, she might understand him a little better.

He once had an older brother called Rowland, and their father was not a nice man. He did not want to split the family fortune up between the two sons, and decided that everything should go to Rowland. He didn't want to leave his other son with nothing, however, and decided he should earn his fortune in a wealthy marriage. He was old friends with Mr. Mason, a West Indian merchant, who had a son and a daughter. Mr. Mason would give his daughter thirty thousand pounds if she married Mr. Rochester. His father said nothing about the money, and only told him that Miss Mason was a beautiful woman. She was similar to Miss Blanche Ingram in many ways — majestic, and tall. He had few private conversations with her and they spent most of their time together at parties. The men in the community admired her, and, because he was so young, Mr. Rochester thought he was in love with her. He found himself married before he knew what was going on. Looking back, he realized he did not know her or love her. He had never met Miss Mason's mother, and thought that she was dead. He learned soon enough that she was in an asylum because she was mad. There was also a younger, dumb brother. Mr. Rochester's family had not considered any of this — they had only thought about the thirty thousand pounds. Mr. Rochester discovered his wife's tastes were completely opposite to his own, and he could not spend a single comfortable hour with her. Every time he tried to talk to her about something, the conversation would turn into a difficult, idiotic one. He realized that he would not have a calm household, either, because no servant would put up with her extreme temper, violent nature or odd orders. Mr. Rochester repressed his resentment for her. He lived with her for four years, during which her behaviour grew worse. Nothing but violence would have curbed her behaviour, and Mr. Rochester did not want to strike her. In these four years, Rowland and his father died.

Mr. Rochester was now rich enough, but he could not get rid of his wife. Doctors had discovered that she was insane. He stopped the story momentarily — Jane offered him her pity, and he accepted it. He continued on: he was depressed, but decided to remove his wife from his sight. Unfortunately, society still associated his name with hers, and this only reminded him of her. One night he woke up to the sound of her screams in the middle of a storm. Mr. Rochester heard Bertha talking in a demon-like way, and he decided he had a right to ease his suffering. He took his pistol out, intending on shooting himself and decided against it moments later. When a fresh European wind blew the storm away, Mr. Rochester decided it was a message. He had to go back to England, confine his mad wife in Thornfield, and live his life how he wanted to. He had suffered enough by his wife's hands, that she was no longer his wife. He would make sure she was well cared for, but keep her a secret. This had been his father's wish, too. After Mr. Rochester sent him a letter about his new wife, his father had become nervous about others finding out about the marriage. Mr. Rochester took his wife to England. She had spent the last ten years in the third storey room. At first, he had found it difficult to find someone to take care of her but finally found Grace Poole. Sometimes Bertha would take advantage of Grace and manage to escape her room, for example on the night when she tried to burn Mr. Rochester's bedroom down and when she visited Jane the night before their wedding.

When he had settled Bertha at Thornfield, he escaped England and went travelling to find a good, intelligent woman to replace his wife with. He was determined to remarry, although he did not want to deceive anybody. He had intended on telling Jane about his wife and never expected the woman he loved to misunderstand his situation. Before he met Jane, he occasionally found a woman he was slightly interested in, but he did not feel that he deserved happiness yet. He could not live alone, though, so tried to take on a mistress. He chose Celine Varens first, and he has already told Jane what happened with her. There were two others, but their beauty bored him after a few months. Jane admits that she doesn't like him as much as she used to and asks if he ever thought the way he was living his life was wrong. Mr. Rochester didn't like it because it wasn't quite living. Hiring a mistress was like having a slave, to him. Jane wondered, if she did give into his request to live together, how long it would take for him to think of her in the same way he thought of his past mistresses.

Last January, filled with bitter despair, he decided to return to England when business called him back. He expected not to find pleasure at Thornfield Hall, and when he passed Jane sitting on the stile, he had no idea she would have such an effect on him. He felt something new that evening. The next day he watched her for half an hour while she played with Adele and marvelled at her patience. Once Adele was tired, Jane went to the window, and Mr. Rochester watched the pleasure she had staring out at the snow. When she was called away by Mrs. Fairfax, Mr. Rochester longed for the evening so he could call her into his presence. He wanted to get to know Jane better. He was pleased and surprised by her daring, keen intelligence and her strength of character. He kept her at arms length to make his investigation of her take longer. He was also worried that Jane would lose her originality if he pushed her too hard. Mr. Rochester wondered if she would come to find him if he pushed her away and was surprised to find that she did not. He often wondered what she thought of him, if she did, and decided to find out by paying more attention to her. He allowed himself to be kind to her, and he watched as her expressions grew softer and happier. He often caught her looking at him, wondering if he was the stern master or the gentle friend. Jane told him not to talk about the old days any longer — it was difficult to hear it knowing what she had to do.

Mr. Rochester announced that he had finally found the woman he had been looking for — the love he had been looking for — and he had found it in Jane. He knew it was cowardly not to tell her about Bertha, but he wanted to make sure Jane was his before he confided his secrets in her. Jane kept silent. She wanted to be loved more than anything in the world, and Mr. Rochester loved her, but she could not stay. She told Mr. Rochester that she would not be his. Mr. Rochester asked her again and again if she really meant it. She did. He asked her what he should do — where he might find a friend. Jane told him to look to God. Mr. Rochester accused her of taking love and happiness from him, throwing him into a life of sin and suffering. Jane had done nothing to him to cause his suffering. He had done that himself, and would forget her in time. Jane was tempted to forgive and live with him, but she would keep her self respect and refuse him. Mr. Rochester saw that he could not persuade her otherwise and his anger rose. He pulled her into his arms and shook her, reminding her that he could break her. He didn't just want her to physically come with him, he also wanted her spirit as well. Finally he let go of her and looked at her. Jane knew if she was far more idiotic, she would have given in, but instead she went to the door. Mr. Rochester asked if she was leaving. Jane was. It was hard for her to keep to her decision, especially when he continued to try and make her feel guilty, but she did not give in. Mr. Rochester gave his consent for her to leave, but only if she kept in mind how much pain she was putting him through. He ordered her to go to her room and think about what he had said. He then threw himself on the sofa and began to cry. Jane walked away from the door and knelt beside him. She kissed his cheek and blessed her master, hoping that God would keep him from suffering and give him a reward for his kindness to her. He only wanted Jane's love. He held his arms out to embrace her, but Jane avoided him and left the room at once.

Jane did not think she would be able to sleep that night, but fell asleep as soon as she lay down. She dreamed about her childhood and the red room at Gateshead. The light that had been in the room moved to the ceiling. Jane looked, and the ceiling opened up to clouds, and then the clouds opened up to the moon. A human form waved the moon away and then spoke to Jane. It told her to escape temptation. Jane woke up and told the figure she would. It was still night time, but Jane got up and put her shoes on, already still dressed from the day before. She packed up her things, but left some items — like the pearl necklace — because they had been gifts from Mr. Rochester and she did not think of them as her own. She made up a small parcel of things, put on her shawl and bonnet, and then escaped from her room. She whispered goodbyes to Mrs. Fairfax and Adele as she passed their rooms, and then came to Mr. Rochester's chamber. Her heart made her stop at the door. He was walking back and forth in his room and sighed. If Jane wanted to, she only had to step in the room and tell him she loved him and they would be wrapped up in a temporary paradise. Jane knew he was waiting until the morning when he could send for her, but he would not find her. Jane's hand moved toward the lock, but she caught herself and moved on. She went into the kitchen and oiled the key and lock, picked up some water and bread, opened the door and shut it behind her quietly. She stepped through a wicket in the gate, and was finally out of Thornfield.

Jane walked down a road she had often passed by but had never travelled. She had always wondered where it had gone and now she would find out. When the sun rose, it was a lovely summer's morning, but she gave no thought to her surroundings. She could only think about her escape and the pain of what she had left. She could not help but think about Mr. Rochester, who would still be hopeful that Jane would change her mind. She still had a chance to run back to the house and comfort him. His fear of abandonment was worse than her own, and it hurt her considerably. Birds began to sing, which reminded her that birds were faithful to their other halves, and symbols of love. She did not know what she was—she hated herself. She cried, walking without seeing, and suddenly went weak. She fell on the ground and lay there for a minute. She hoped and feared that she might die there and then, but suddenly found herself crawling on hands and knees, and then on her feet, eager to reach the road. She sat under a hedge for a moment to rest. A coach came up the road and Jane put her hand out to stop it. She asked where it was going—it was going far away, to a place Jane was sure Mr. Rochester would have no connections to. Although the driver wanted 30 shillings and Jane only had 20 shillings to her name, he still let her get inside the coach, which was empty, and it rolled away. Jane hoped that her readers would never have to think of themselves as evil to the person they really love.

Chapter Twenty-Eight:

Two days passed and Jane found herself out of the coach in a place called Whitecross. The driver could not take her any further with her smaller sum of money, and Jane had no other shillings to her name. She was alone. Jane discovered that she had left her parcel of things in the coach. She was now completely poor. Whitecross was not a town or hamlet, but a stone pillar where four roads met. Jane learned from the signposts that she was in a northern area surrounded by moors and mountains. The population of this area would be small, and there were no people on the roads. Jane did not want to see strangers — they might wonder what she was doing, and then she would be questioned. Nothing she would say in response would avoid suspicion — she had no relatives, no friends, so she would have to go back into the depths of the natural world. She waded through thick grass and then sat underneath a mossy rocky ledge. It took a long time before Jane calmed down — she thought every sound she heard was a person or a wild animal. She did not know where to go or what to do, or when her suffering might end. She looked around and thought that nature loved her — it was good, and pure, and not at all like man who might reject her. She had a small piece of bread left and saw some berries nearby. She ate them both, and then said her prayers before lying down to sleep. She longed for Mr. Rochester, and could not sleep for her longing. She got onto her knees and looked around at the night sky. She felt God's presence when she looked upon the grand sky, and felt his might and strength. Although she had risen to her knees to pray for Mr. Rochester, she knew she did not have to. He would be well protected. She thanked God, and then disappeared into a deep sleep.

The next day, Jane marvelled at the hot sunshine and wished she could live in it — maybe as a lizard. However, being human, she had a human's wants and could not stay in a place that would not protect her. She had hoped that God would have taken her soul while she slept because her future was such a hopeless one, but she was obviously still alive and she had to continue on, suffering or not. She went back to the road and walked away from the sun.

When she had walked a long time, she sat on a stone to rest for a moment and heard a bell chime. It was a church bell, and Jane turned around to look at it. A small village and a Church lay in the hills, and a waggon, two cows and their driver were going up the hill. Jane had to reach the village, so she got up and pushed on. She entered the village and came across a small shop with bread in the window. She wanted something to eat so she could replenish her energy, but she did not have any money on her. She did have her silk handkerchief and gloves, but she did not know if they would accept them in lieu of payment. When she entered the shop, a lady came toward her and asked how she could serve Jane. She obviously expected to be able to sell her something, but Jane could not say anything. She was ashamed, and froze for a moment. She only asked permission to sit down for a moment. The lady showed her to a seat, disappointed. Jane wanted to cry, but refused to let herself. She asked about employment in the village, but there were no jobs available, and most places did not hire women. A few other people stepped in and Jane's chair was needed, so she left. Jane went up the street, looking at all the houses, but she could find no reason why she would go up to them. She went up to a pretty house and knocked on the door to ask if they needed a servant, but none was needed. Jane asked if she had any news of employment anywhere, but the woman could not give her any information. If she had kept the door open to Jane a little longer, Jane would have begged for a piece of bread. She continued to wander the village like a lost dog. She came to the Church and asked if the clergyman was in, but he was out, called away by the sudden death of his own father. Jane went back to the shop and asked the lady there if she would swap her handkerchief or gloves for a piece of bread, but the lady did not know what she would do with them, or where they had come from. Jane did not blame any of the people who sent her away — it was what was expected, especially as a finely dressed beggar raised suspicion.

Just before dark, Jane passed a farm house. A farmer sat in front of an open door eating bread and cheese. She asked him if she could have a piece of bread, and the farmer cut her a thick slice. Jane took it, sat out of sight of the house and ate it. She knew she could not sleep under a roof, but the wood was damp and cold, and she had to move multiple times in the night to avoid being found. It rained towards morning and throughout the next day. She continued to look for work, and starved. She did find food when a girl was about to throw cold porridge into a pig's trough. The girl's mother let her have it if she was a beggar, and Jane ate it quickly from her hands. Jane continued walking until sunset again, and felt that she could not go any further. She was very weak and thought she would die before morning. She did not want to, especially when she remembered Mr. Rochester was still alive. She looked around and knew that she had walked far away from the village, but she was happy because she would rather die in the country than in the street. She turned toward a hill and tried to find a cave to lie down in, but the country was level. As she looked over it, she suddenly saw a light and wondered if it was a light in the window of a house. She did not want to walk toward it at first because she was afraid they would shut the door in her face, but she finally pushed herself to walk through the rain. She fell twice, but the light kept her going.

Soon she came to a house, surrounded by a white gate. Jane wondered if the inhabitants had already gone to bed. She looked through the un-shuttered window into the house, and discovered an elderly woman knitting my candlelight. Two young, graceful women sat near the fireplace, one with a dog in her lap, and the other with a cat in her lap. Jane knew that these delicate women couldn't be the daughters of the elderly lady, and thought that the setting was a strange one for them. They were not beautiful ladies — their intense concentration with their books made them look severe and hard. After a moment of silence, one of the ladies told her companion about the characters in the book they were reading, and then read something in a different language. Jane knew it was not French or Latin, but a different language. Her companion repeated one of the lines read aloud and shared her appreciation for it. The old woman asked them about the language and where it was spoken. She thought the young ladies would be able to understand it if they went to the country. One of the young ladies argued that they were not as smart as she thought they were — they needed a dictionary to understand German. They planned to teach it at some point so they could earn more money. The old lady, who was called Hannah, told them to stop studying for the night, and the two ladies agreed. They wondered when St. John would come home. Hannah went to check on the fire in another room and returned to express her sadness that the room was empty, and the chair was sat in the corner. Clearly someone had died, as Hannah agreed that he was in a better place and had a quiet death. The man they had lost was the ladies' father and had died very quickly — too quickly for them to be sent for in time.

The two ladies, Mary and Diana, stood and went into the parlour while Hannah started to prepare their supper. Jane suddenly remembered her situation and went to the door to knock on it, even though she did not think she should disturb them with her own problems. Hannah opened the door and Jane asked to speak to the young ladies. She wanted to sleep with a roof over her head and a small bit of bread to eat. Hannah would not let her into the house, but she would give her something to eat. She also wouldn't let Jane speak to the mistresses. Jane did not know where she would go if she went away. Hannah didn't really care where she would go — she was sure that Jane knew where she was going to go, and offered her a penny. Jane begged her not to close the door — she didn't have the strength to continue walking. She would died if she was turned away. Hannah accused her of wanting to commit a crime, possibly as part of a team, and told her to send a message to her cohorts that a gentleman, dog and a gun lay in the house. Hanna closed and bolted the door behind her. Jane could not take it anymore. She fell to her knees and sobbed. Her hope was gone for a moment, and then she remembered she would go to God if she died. A voice told her that all men would died, but not all would be condemned to an early death. Jane asked who was speaking. A man stepped forward and knocked on the door. This was Mr. St. John. He told Hannah to open the door. She warned him against the beggar woman and told Jane to get away from the house. Mr. St. John told Hannah she had done her job in protecting the house, but it was his job to now admit her into the house. He was nearby when he heard them talking, and he thought Jane's case was an unusual one. He told Jane to stand and follow him into the house. The inhabitants stared at her. They thought Jane was very pale. She started to faint and they gave her a chair to sit on.

Jane recovered a little, but could not speak. They gave her some water and bread, and wondered if she was ill. Diana broke off some bread, dipped it in milk and held it to Jane's lips. Mary encouraged her to eat, and they both looked very sympathetic. Mary took off her sodden bonnet and helped her sister. When Jane had eaten a little, St. John asked for her name, which she gave as Jane Elliot, eager to avoid giving her real name. When they wondered if there was anyone they could send for, Jane shook her head. He asked how Jane had come to the house, but she would not provide him with any details that night. He wondered what she expected him to do, but Jane expected nothing from them. Diana asked if she meant that she had received the aid she needed and would go back out into the moor. Jane smiled and told her she trusted them not to send her out into the world, but they could do with her what she wanted. They gave her a bit more food, while St. John, Mary and Diana went into the parlour to talk. One of the ladies returned after a while, but Jane could not tell which as she was falling into a stupor. The lady whispered directions to Hannah, and Jane found herself led up the stairs. Her wet clothes were removed, and she was put into a warm, dry bed. Jane thanked God and fell into an exhausted sleep.

Chapter Twenty-Nine:

Jane could not remember much of the next three days and nights. She knew she was in bed, and if she had been taken from it, she would have died. She did not know how long she had been there, and if someone entered her room she did not even know who it was. She understood what was said to her, but could not answer. Opening her lips or moving her limbs were equally difficult things to do. Hannah was her most frequent visitor, but hers was a disturbing presence. Jane was sure that Hannah wanted her to go away, and did not understand her. Diana and Mary would whisper to one another in Jane's presence that they were pleased that they took her in. They knew she was educated and probably quite pretty when she was not famished, and never uttered a word of regret at taking her in. St. John came only once to tell her that her illness was due to exhaustion but she had no disease and would heal in time. Diana commented that she hoped to house Jane on a more permanent basis, but St. John disagreed—he thought they would find out that she was a lady who had disagreed with her friends and would return to them.

On the third day Jane was much better and on the fourth she could speak and sit up in bed. Hannah gave her some food to eat and she felt much stronger. She decided she would dress, but worried about putting on her dirty clothes. When she looked over at the chair she saw her things clean and dry. Her clothes were a lot looser because of the weight she had lost, but she was once more clean and respectable. She went down the stairs and found a fire burning while Hannah baked. Hannah had started to trust her a little more, and she smiled when she saw that Jane was up and about, and sent her to sit by the fire. She asked Jane if she had ever begged before. Jane told her she wasn't a beggar, but Hannah didn't understand: did she have a home or money? Jane told her that the absence of neither of those things made a beggar. Hannah discovered that she was well educated and wondered why she did not have a job to earn a living with. Jane admitted she had managed to support herself before and would be able to do it again.

Jane asked to help her make the pies, and Hannah allowed her to do so. She commented that Jane had not performed servant's work—she could tell by Jane's hands. Jane told her not to worry about what she had been doing and to tell her what the house was called. It was called Marsh End by some, and Moor House by others. St. John did not live in the house and only stayed a while. He had his own parish in Morton, the village a few miles away. His father, Mr. Rivers, lived in this house and had died of a stroke. Hannah had been with the family for thirty years. Jane knew that she must be an honest, faithful servant if she had, even though she did call Jane a beggar. Jane told her that not even a dog should have been sent away from the door during a night like that, let alone a person. Hannah admitted that it had been hard, but what else could she do but think of her two young ladies. She had to protect them. Jane admitted she did not think much of Hannah because she judged people who did not have a house or money—some of the best people were as poor as Jane was, and if she was a Christian she should not think of poverty as a crime. Hannah admitted she had been told as much by St. John and knew she was wrong. Jane forgave her and they shook hands. From that moment they were friends.

Hannah talked about the family while they made the pies. Mr. Rivers was a member of an ancient family who had lived at Marsh End since it was built. Even though Hannah thought of him as a gentleman, he still liked shooting and farming. His wife was an avid reader and her daughters had taken after her. The two ladies found places as governesses as their father had lost their fortune and they had to provide for themselves. They had not lived in the house recently, and had only returned because of their father's death. Jane asked where St. John and the ladies were right at that moment. They had gone to Morton for a walk, but would return soon enough. When they did return, they came into the kitchen. St. John bowed to Jane and moved on, but Mary and Diana stopped to tell her how pleased they were that she was up and about. Diana had wanted her to wait until she said Jane was well enough to move as she was still quite pale and thin. Of the two sisters, Diana was the most authoritative and Mary was gentler. Diana wondered what she was doing in the kitchen. She and her sister sat in it every now and then, but Jane was a visitor and had to sit in the parlour. Jane liked the kitchen, but Diana didn't think it was right for her to be covered in flour. She made Jane stand and then led her into the parlour. Diana left her for a moment with St. John while she went to make tea with her sister.

St. John read quietly while Jane looked around her at the plainly furnished room. St. John was still quite young and had a classically handsome look to him. He did not say a single word to her. Diana returned with the tea and gave her a little cake to eat. St. John closed his book and studied her. He stated that she was obviously hungry, and should eat now that her fever had gone. Jane hoped that she would not have to eat at their expense for too long. St. John told her that she could be on her way once she handed them her friend's address. Jane admitted she had no home and no friends. They all looked at her but without suspicion. St. John asked her to confirm she had no connections at all, and Jane admitted she had no one. He looked at Jane's hands, and then asked if she was a widow, or if she had been married. Diana laughed at him on account of Jane's age — she couldn't be a spinster! Jane admitted she was nineteen and had not been married. She could not help but blush at her memory of Mr. Rochester, and they all saw her embarrassment. St. John asked where she lived last, but Jane told them it was a secret she would not reveal to them. Diana agreed she had a right to keep that information to herself, but St. John could not help her if she gave them no information about her past. Jane needed help, but she only needed help finding work. St. John would help her with this.

He asked her what she had experience with. Jane swallowed her tea and gathered strength enough to admit that she would tell them anything she could about her past without upsetting herself. She told them about Lowood, her governess position and her need to leave that position. She assured them she would not reveal the reason for her departure, but she was not to blame for the situation that she found herself in there. She told them about the coach to Whitecross, her loss of her parcel, the walk with the village and her two days of starvation. When Diana told Jane to sit with her on the sofa because she was obviously tired, she called Jane by her alias "Jane Elliot". Jane reacted, having forgotten her alias at first, and St. John noticed. He asked her about it, and she admitted that it was not her real name, but the name she wanted to be referred to at first. Her real name might lead to discoveries about her identity and past. Diana and Mary demanded that she stay with them, and St. John had no other choice but to agree with them until he could find Jane a job. He had a small circle of acquaintances and friends, and it might take him a little while. Jane would do anything—even if it meant she had to be a servant. St. John promised to help her in his own time and way. He returned to his book, and Jane left the room, tired from talking too much.

Chapter Thirty:

The better Jane got to know the people of Moor House, the more she liked them. In a few days, she had enough strength to sit up all day and even walk around outside sometimes. She helped Diana and Mary with their occupations, talked with them as much as they wanted to, and it helped Jane to get better. She loved their home, and their studies. She loved the books they read and the countryside around the house. The two ladies were more accomplished and more broadly educated than she was, but she followed their pursuit of knowledge, devoured the books they lent to her, and discussed them with the ladies in the evening. Diana was their natural leader: she was physically beautiful and her personality exuded confidence. She offered to teach German to Jane, and Jane loved learning from her. The sisters and Jane became great friends and students of the same subjects, but St. John did not extend the same intimacy her way. He was rarely at home and spent most of his time visiting the sick and poor in his parish. No matter the weather, he would put his hat on after his morning studies and go out into the world. If the weather was very bad, his sisters would ask him to stay home, but he refused; if poor weather kept him from his easy work, what would his future be like? There was another barrier to their friendship in his reserved, brooding personality. He seemed troubled and did not have the internal contentedness that most Christians expected of their souls. Nature did not excite the same admiration in him that it did in Jane and the two sisters, and he never went for a walk to soothe his feelings. He only walked for his work. Jane did not understand St. John's mind until she attended a sermon in his Morton Church. She wished she could properly describe the sermon, but it was beyond her power to do so. It was a fairly calm sermon, but it excited Jane's mind and heart. He touched on his disappointment with fate and sin regularly, and Jane found herself sadder than before it began instead of enlightened by it. She knew St. John experienced great doubt and disappointment, and was sure he had not yet found the peace that God and faith were meant to bring him.

A month had gone by, and Diana and Mary were about to leave Moor House for their positions as governesses in southern England for wealthy families. St John had said nothing about the search for employment for Jane, and it became more urgent that she find something to do. One minute, while alone with him, she asked him if he had found something for her. He admitted he had found something for her three weeks ago but she had seemed so happy with his sisters that he didn't dare mention it until their departure from Moor House. In three days time the two sisters would leave, St. John would return to his parsonage at Morton and Hannah would go with him. Moor House would be locked up. Jane waited for a few moments, expecting him to continue, but his mind wandered and Jane had to prompt him. She wondered if their delay would mean she would lose the employment, but St. John admitted he was going to employ her. He told her it would not be affluent work because he had little to nothing to his own name. He thought she would find it degrading work, especially as he had watched her and knew her tastes were more educated and suited to higher classes. St. John believed that nothing a man could do to help his own race was degrading work, and the harder the work, the more honourable it was. He continued to take a long while between his statements and studied Jane's face the whole time. He was sure that Jane would accept the post and hold it for awhile, but not permanently. He would leave Morton in about a year now that he was his own master, but he wanted to improve it before he left. It had no school when he arrived and he established one for boys shortly after arriving. He wanted to open one for girls and had already hired a building for it. It was a cottage, with two rooms for the mistress. Jane's salary would be thirty pounds a year, and she already had furniture in the house waiting for her. Miss Oliver, the wife of the factory owner in the valley, paid for the education and clothing of orphans from the workhouses as long as the mistress would help her out with tasks that did not get in the way of her teaching.

St. John seemed to expect a refusal as he rushed the explanation. It was a poorer job, but she would be more independent than a governess in a rich house. It was also not an unworthy position. She accepted it. St. John made sure she understood that her students would be poor, uneducated children. He wondered what she would do with her other talents and accomplishments. Jane explained they would still keep, and that she understood what she would do. She would go to her house the next day and then open the school the following week. As St. John went to leave the room, he turned and shook his head at her. He did not think she would stay at Morton long. Jane would — she was not ambitious. At first, St. John thought she was calling him ambitious. He thought that her long working hours without intellectual stimulation and living in solitude would affect her. He knew what restlessness felt like even though he had God's work to do. He left the room. Jane was more confused by him than ever.

Diana and Mary became sadder as the day for their departure approached. It would be a different kind of separation for them — they might not see one another again for years, or even for life. It broke their heart that they would lose their home as they had lost their father. St. John passed them, then, and told them that he had received word that their Uncle John had died too. Mary and Diana read the letter quietly, and then smiled at one another. Diana commented that they could live, Mary thought they were no worse off than they were before, and St. John reminded them that things might have been very different and then left. Diana explained that they were not so heartless to be pleased by a relative's death. He was their mother's brother, and he had ruined their father's fortune by persuading him into business. They parted in anger, and their Uncle managed to raise a small fortune of twenty thousand pounds. He was never married and had no other true relations except for one. Their father had always hoped that the fortune would be left to them to make up for what their Uncle had done, but the letter revealed he had left it to the other relation. He only left thirty guineas to his nieces and nephews to buy mourning rings for each of them. The money would have made them comfortable and allowed St. John to do more good for the community, but none of it would go to them. The subject was dropped after this and no more references were made by any of the family. Jane left Moor House the next day, Diana and Mary left the day after, and in a week St. John and Hannah left for the parsonage.

Chapter Thirty-One:

Jane's home was a cottage with white washed walls, sanded floors and a collection of furniture. The school had opened that morning, and Jane had just sent the little orphan, who was serving as her handmaid, home. There were twenty students, but only three could read, and none of them could write. Some of them could knit and very few could sew, and Jane found it very difficult to understand their accents. While some students had no manners and were rough and ignorant, others had a desire to learn and a gentle disposition. Jane had to remind herself that the children were flesh and blood and that all of them had the capacity for intelligence and kind feelings, and her duty was to coax this out of them. Jane did not expect to find much joy in her job, but if she kept track of how she felt and regulated her feelings, she would be able to survive day to day.

Despite her enthusiasm, Jane did feel lonely and degraded. She felt she had taken a step which sunk her in the social ladder, and was upset by the poor, ignorant people around her. She knew her feelings to be wrong, however, and would work hard to overcome them. In a few months she might even be happier when she saw progress in her students. She wondered if her life with Mr. Rochester as a foolish slave to love would have been worse or better than her life as an honest and free village schoolmistress. She knew she was right to keep to her principles and step away from her frenzied emotions. She felt God had directed her to the right choice and place in life and thanked him for his guidance. She watched the sunset and found herself happy, but crying. She wept for Mr. Rochester and the harm and sin he might be putting himself into because of her escape. Jane rested her head against the door frame until a slight noise from the gate made her look up. Carlos, St. John's dog, pushed against the gate with his nose and St. John leaned on it. He looked troubled, almost displeased.

She asked him to come in. He couldn't—he had only come to deliver a small parcel of pencils, paper and colours from his sister. While she came close to accept it, Jane knew he could see the evidence of tears on her face. He asked her if she found her first day quite hard. Jane thought she would get on with her students very well in time. He then asked about her accommodations, but she interrupted to tell him she was very thankful for them. Five weeks before, she had nothing to her name. She thought God's goodness and her friend's generosity was wonderful. He wondered if she was lonely. Jane had not had time to feel it yet. St. John was pleased. He advised her to resist every temptation to look back at her past, whatever it was, and to continue pursuing her current endeavours. He knew it was difficult to control impulsive actions, but God had given them the power to make their own fates. He had been miserable a year before when he suspected entering the ministry was a mistake. He longed for a more active, exciting life and thought he had to change his life or die. After struggling for a while, he heard a call from Heaven delivering God's mission for his life. He had to be a missionary: combining his ministry work with that of a soldier's and politician's. Although his father disliked his proposed path, St. John had vowed he would overcome his weakness and leave England for the East.

They stared up at the setting sun while he spoke and did not hear footsteps come toward them. A voice called out a greeting to St. John, who was known as Mr. Rivers to this person, and to the dog. The woman was dressed in pure white and had a youthful, graceful form. She threw her veil back to reveal a beautiful face. Jane had never seen such a flawless face, and she admired her with her entire heart. Jane wondered what St. John thought of this angel and looked at him. He barely looked at her as he told her it was too late for her to be out alone. He crushed flowers beneath his foot. She told him she had come from a nearby town that afternoon and she wanted to see the new school and mistress. She asked Jane if she would like Morton. Jane hoped she would. The woman asked if she had furnished it nicely for her use, and Jane thought that this was Miss Oliver, the heiress. She told Jane she would come to help teach the students sometimes as it would be a change of pace for her every now and then. She mentioned that she had been happy lately, especially as here had been a dance the previous night where the officers of a regiment had attended. Jane thought St. John's face looked quite stern as he listened to this. He turned and looked at her, and she laughed. He did not speak, and she commented that his dog was far friendlier, especially if he was going to remain silent.

As she patted the dog, St. John's face glowed with sudden emotion. Jane thought he looked quite handsome, then. Miss Oliver commented that he did not come to visit them at Vale Hall anymore, and that he should return with her to visit her sick father. St. John would not visit them so late at night, but Miss Oliver wanted him to come — it was exactly the time of day when her father would like company. She wondered why he was shy and sad and then suddenly remembered that his sisters were gone and Moor House was closed up. He told her he would not visit that night, calling her Miss Rosamond. Jane knew it had taken great effort for him to say no to her. She would not dare stay any longer as the night was approaching and said goodbye to them both. She returned for a moment to ask St. John if he was well, her own face as pale as her gown. He told her he was well and then left the gate. She went away in the other direction, turning around twice to look back at him. He strode on, never looking back. Witnessing someone sacrificing and suffering drew Jane away from thoughts about her own suffering.

Chapter Thirty-Two:

Jane continued to teach at the village school as well and faithfully as she could. It was hard work at first and it took some time before her efforts made any difference in the students and their natures. They had seemed dull to her, without hope of changing, but Jane found she was wrong. There were differences among all of them, and when she got to know the properly she realized that they were sharp and witty girls. Most of them were friendly, polite and self-respecting, and these traits earned Jane's goodwill and admiration. Most of them took pleasure in working well, keeping themselves neat and tidy, and learning their tasks properly. Some of them excelled at their work at a very quick pace, and it surprised Jane. Some of the best girls in the school liked Jane very much, and she liked them too. There were several farmer's daughters at her school who were already young women and could already read, write and sew. Jane taught these girls the elements of grammar, geography, history and finer kinds of needlework. These girls wanted to improve and to learn, and Jane often found herself spending hours at their homes with their families. Jane enjoyed accepting their kindness, and the farmers seemed to enjoy accepting her attention. It made them feel wanted and a little more important. Jane soon became one of the neighbourhood's favourites. Many people said hello to her as they passed and most smiled at her. Jane was very thankful for her life — living among the working class and being welcomed by them made her happy. At night, however, she had strange dreams about adventure and romance, always meeting Mr. Rochester in the middle of some sort of exciting moment and ending up in his arms. When she woke up from these dreams she was quite sad, but she was calm and settled by the time she had to open up the school.

Rosamond Oliver kept her promise to visit the school. She would generally visit in the morning during St. John's daily Christian lesson. Jane could see a difference in him when she stepped into the room, even if he didn't realize it himself — his cheeks would glow and his features would change to more expressive ones. While Rosamond knew she had power over him, St. John obviously did not because he could not conceal it from her. His hands would tremble and he would smile when she spoke to him. Even though he did not say the words, his behaviour seemed to say to her that he loved her, but his heart had already been pledged to God and Heaven. She would seem to realize this, pout and then withdraw from her St. John, the martyr. He would not give up his missionary life in favour of the peace and quiet of Vale Hall. Jane knew this first hand from St. John when he confided in her one day.

After multiple visits, Jane knew a lot about Miss Oliver. She had been indulged since her birth, but had not been spoiled. She was vain, charming, innocent, friendly and unthinking. She was not interesting or impressive enough for Jane, and her mind was very different to that possessed by St. John and his sisters. She liked her as much as she had liked Adele, except she had a deeper affection for the child. Miss Oliver commented that Jane was a little like her Mr. Rivers, but not as beautiful. She thought Jane was good, clever and firm like him, however, and thought that her mysterious past would make for a fantastic romance tale. One day she went rummaging through Jane's things and discovered her French and German books and her pictures. She was delighted and surprised by these discoveries and asked her if she would sketch a portrait of her for her father. Jane was delighted she had such a beautiful, perfect model as a subject. She drew a careful outline but could not finish it that night. She made Miss Oliver promise to come back so she could finish colouring it. Her father, after hearing about Jane's abilities, accompanied her the next night. He was a large, tall, middle aged man. He seemed quite proud, but was nice to Jane. Rosamond's portrait pleased him and he insisted that she should finish it, and then visit Vale Hall the next evening.

Vale Hall was a large house. Mr. Oliver commented that Jane was too good for her school and worried that she would leave for somewhere far more suitable in time. Rosamond thought she was clever enough to be a governess in a wealthy family, but Jane would rather be where she was. Mr. Oliver spoke about the Rivers family with a deep respect. Theirs was an old, respectable name in the area, and their ancestors had been wealthy. He thought that the representative of the house, i.e., St. John, might make an alliance with the best family in the area. He thought his decision to become a missionary was a waste of a good man's valuable life. Jane knew then that Mr. Oliver approved of a match between his daughter and St. John, and obviously did not care that there was no fortune to be had from him.

On the 5th November, a holiday, her home had just been cleaned up her handmaid for a penny. Jane tidied herself up and had the day to spend as she wanted. She translated some German for a while and then completed Rosamond Oliver's portrait. She was so absorbed in her work that she did not hear St. John Rivers step into the room. He had come to see how she was spending her holiday and was pleased that she was drawing. It would keep her from feeling lonely: despite the fact that she had managed with her new life, he still worried that she was alone. He gave her a book to spend the holiday with. While she spent a few moments looking at the pages of poetry, St. John looked at her drawing. He said nothing, but Jane knew what he thought about. She decided to try and do him some good if she could and talk to him about Rosamond. She told him to sit down, but he told her he couldn't stay, as he always did. Jane had concluded solitude was just as bad for him as it was for her and decided to discover more about him.

She asked him if the drawing was a good likeness for the living thing, and when he argued he had not looked at it enough, she placed it in his hands to do exactly that. Jane told him that she would paint him a copy of the picture if he admitted to her that he would appreciate the gift. He continued to look at the picture, complimenting the eyes, expression and smile. They were exactly like Rosamond's. She wondered if it would give him pain or comfort to have her painting with him when he went away. He would like to have it but did not know if it would be wise to do so. After her visit to Vale Hall, Jane had concluded that St. John would do more good if he inherited the Oliver fortune and married Rosamond. She persuaded him to take the original picture for himself at once. He sat down and placed the picture on the table in front of him and continued to study it. Instead of angry with Jane for being so honest and direct about his love for Rosamond, he seemed to take pleasure in hearing about it out loud. Jane told him that Rosamond liked him and that her father approved and respected him. Jane thought he ought to marry her. He liked to hear that she liked him and told Jane to talk about it for fifteen minutes. He placed a watch on the table to measure the time accurately. Jane didn't think it was useful for her to talk for that long when he would think up a contradiction or rejection of the marriage. St. John told her not to imagine that he might be that stubborn. He still imagined what it might be like if he married her — he would be endlessly happy.

When the fifteen minutes was up, he placed the watch back in his pocket and stood, leaving the picture on the table. If he was led into temptation, her promises to him would be empty and false ones. He loved Rosamond Oliver, especially as she was fascinating and beautiful, but she would not make a good wife. He knows he would discover this within the first year of marriage to her, and would regret it for the rest of his life. Rosamond would not suffer being a missionary's wife. Jane argued he wouldn't need to be a missionary, but St. John wouldn't dream of giving up Heaven's great plan for his life. He wanted to carry knowledge into the world, especially into the depths of ignorant races. Exchanging superstition for religion and replacing the fear of hell with the hope of heaven would be a task he could not give up. It was dearer to him than the blood in his veins. Jane wondered if Miss Oliver's disappointment meant anything to him. He thought she would marry and forget him and would be far happier than she would have been with him. Jane argued that the thought of this upset him, but St. John was only anxious about his own future. He wanted to get on with his life, and had heard only that morning that his replacement would not be able to take over from him for at least three months. Jane pointed out that he blushed and trembled when Miss Oliver stepped into the schoolroom. St. John was surprised by her honesty, but Jane felt at home speaking the way she did. While he applauded her braveness, he argued that she thought his emotions were far stronger than they actually were. When he trembled near Miss Oliver he hated the weakness of his body. His soul did not tremble. He argued that reason was his guide rather than emotion, and he only desire to rise higher and do more than other people. For example, he watched Jane's career with interest because she was an orderly, dedicated woman, not because he felt sorry for her past or her suffering. He wanted to spread his religion across the world and achieve victories for it. As for his emotions? He had to suffer through them until his soul went to Heaven.

He looked once more at the portrait. He thought Rosamond was lovely. Jane asked if he wanted a copy, but St. John did not. He took a sheet of thin paper and placed it across the portrait. As he did this, he saw something on the paper which made him pick it up and look a something on the edge. He looked back at Jane with curiosity, placed the paper down and told her that nothing was wrong. He tore a narrow strip from the margin, slipped it into his glove and slipped away. Jane looked at the paper after he had gone, but could not figure out what it was that had caught his attention. She decided it was nothing important and soon forgot the incident.

Chapter Thirty-Three:

It had begun to snow just after St. John left the cottage, and the storm continued all night. Jane had taken measures to prevent any snow from entering the cottage and lit a fire to warm her rooms. She had just begun to read when St. John lifted the latch on her door and stepped in. He was covered in snow. Jane demanded if something had happened. Nothing had. He shook the snow off of his cloak and boots and apologized for making her home a little dirtier, but she had to excuse him this once. He told her it had been hard work making his way to her cottage — the snow was waist deep in some areas! Jane wondered why he had come. He wanted to talk to her after he had grown bored of his books and empty rooms. He also wanted the second half of the previous day's story told. He sat down. Jane wondered if St. John had gone mad, but he was very calm and focused. She waited for him to say something she actually understood, but he was already deep in thought. She felt sorry for him and told him she wished Diana and Mary would come back to live with him so they could look after him. St. John didn't see why they would be needed as he took good care of himself.

After a few more moments of silence, Jane told him she would read her book. Soon, St. John removed a letter from his pocket, read it in silence, and placed it back in his pocket. Jane asked him about his sisters, and then about his own plans for the future — he did not think he would be leaving England soon. Jane changed the subject and told him about her students. She would be getting four new girls and two of them would be sponsored by Mr. Oliver. Her students would also be getting a treat at Christmas because Miss Oliver had suggested it. Another pause in the conversation came. St. John told Jane to leave her book alone and come to sit nearer him and the fire. Jane did. St. John reminded her that he had wanted the sequel to a half told story. He thought it would be better if he told the story and she listened to him.

He told her that twenty years prior a curate fell in love with a rich man's daughter. She fell in love with him too, and married him despite the opposition of her friends and family. They disowned her after the ceremony. After two years, the couple were dead and buried side by side, leaving a daughter. She went to the house of rich relatives — her Aunt-in-law, Mrs. Reed. She kept the orphan for ten years and then sent it away to Lowood School, where Jane went herself. Her career was great and became a governess to Mr. Rochester's ward. He did not know anything about Mr. Rochester other than that he had offered marriage to this girl, and that the discovery of his living lunatic wife was made. When they needed to give her information, she could not be found and no one could guess where she had gone, even though they had looked up and down the country. Advertisements were placed in the paper, and St. John had just received a letter from Mr. Briggs detailing the story. He thought it was an odd tale.

Jane asked him if he knew how Mr. Rochester was. He did not, and thought it would be better if she asked him the name of the governess involved instead. She pushed for more information, but there had been no letters from him—only from Alice Fairfax. Jane's suspicions were true ones: he had fled the country for Europe. She pitied him. St. John thought he must have been a bad man, but Jane told him she couldn't judge him if she didn't know him. Since Jane refused to ask the name of the governess, he produced a shabby piece of torn paper. Jane recognized it: it was from her cover. The name "Jane Eyre" was written in the corner. Mr. Briggs had written to him about Jane Eyre, the advertisements demanded Jane Eyre, and even though until the previous day he had only known a Jane Elliot, he had had his suspicions. Jane admitted she was Jane Eyre and asked if Mr. Briggs might know a bit more about Mr. Rochester, but it was not Mr. Rochester he was interested in. He wanted to tell Jane that her uncle, Mr. Eyre of Madeira, was dead and had left her his fortune. She was rich! She only had to prove her identity and the money would be hers. She was happy, but it was still a sobering, solid moment. Her only living relative was dead. She had hoped to meet him, but now she was isolated once again. Her independence made her very happy though. Her fortune was twenty thousand pounds, which almost took Jane's breath away. She had not expected a sum that large! St. John put his cloak back on and stood. He had to leave her alone.

As he lifted the latch, Jane stopped him. She wanted to know how Mr. Briggs had known he should write to St. John. He would have rather that Diana or Mary tell her, but Jane wanted to know immediately. Even if St. John was a hard man, Jane was an equally hard woman. He yielded. He was christened St. John Eyre Rivers. Jane connected the entire story together and realized what this meant before St. John had uttered another word. His mother's name was Eyre and she had two brothers. Mr. Briggs had written to him to tell him about their Uncle's death and that he had left his fortune to his brother's orphaned daughter. He wrote again a few weeks later to tell him that the heiress was missing and asking if he knew anything about her. Again he went to go, but Jane stopped him. Jane double checked: he was her cousin, as was Mary and Diana. Jane looked at him — she had found a brother of sorts, and one she could be proud of and love, and two sisters who, even when they appeared strangers, encouraged admiration and affection. This was the real wealth Jane had found. She had found family! She clapped her hands with joy. St. John told her she neglected more important points for silly ones — she was serious when he told her about her fortune. Jane explained she had no family, and now she had three relatives! She was overcome with thoughts of the future and what she could do for her cousins who protected her from death in her hour of need. She could reunite them in their own independence. Her fortune was theirs — they could split it four ways and still have enough of a fortune each. The wealth no longer weighed on her, but was a beacon of hope.

St. John sat her down in a chair and told her to calm down. Jane told him to write to Mary and Diana the next day — they would have thought themselves rich with a thousand pounds, so she didn't know what they would do when they found they had five thousand pounds each. St. John tried to make her calm down — she was obviously confused. Jane assured him she was perfectly fine. She loved Moor House and wanted to live there with Diana and Mary. It would torment her to have twenty thousand pounds — especially if her Uncle had refused to recognize her cousins — but five thousand pounds would be of benefit to her. St. John urged her to consider the matter for a few days. She was rushing into things. St. John pointed out that the fortune had been earned by his Uncle alone, not through the family line, so it was up to him who to leave it to. Jane wanted to indulge her own feelings on the matter as she had had so few chances to do so in the past. St. John continued to argue that she had no idea what twenty thousand pounds would do for her future, but Jane assured him she had always wanted a home, and wanted a brother and sisters. St. John would be her brother with or without the fortune — Jane wouldn't have that. Mary and Diana would be slaving away in another person's home while St. John would be thousands of miles away from her. He thought she might make her own family when she married, but Jane would never marry. She knew how she felt about these things. No one would take her because of love, and she would not marry someone who only wanted her for her money. St. John respected her principles and mind, liked her presence and her conversation and could easily make room for her in his heart as his third sister. Jane thanked him. She would stay on as the teacher of the school until a replacement could be found. He left.

Jane had to struggle hard to split the fortune the way she wanted it to be, but her cousins saw that she was fixed on this plan and agreed to it. St. John, Diana, Mary and Jane became small fortune holders of five thousand pounds each.

Chapter Thirty-Four:

It was close to Christmas when everything was settled. Jane closed Morton school and had made sure that all of her students knew that she would visit them once a week at least, and to teach for an hour. It was clear that her students were grateful for all she had done for them and had great affection for her. St. John came up to see the students — now sixty girls strong — leave. Jane locked the door and stood talking with a few of her special students. They were some of the most decent, respectable, modest and well-informed young women in the working classes, and that was saying a lot — Jane thought that the working class people were the best in the entirety of Europe. St. John wondered if Jane felt rewarded for her season of work. It gave her great pleasure, but she could not go on. She wanted to enjoy her abilities, mind and body while she still could. She wanted to be as active as possible: she wanted Hannah to come with her to Moor House to get everything in order for Diana and Mary's return in a week. St. John had been worried she was off on an excursion — he was happier that she was staying. Jane gave him the key to the school and would give him the key to her cottage the next day. St. John thought she was far too happy giving it up and wondered what she would do to fill her days. Jane would clean Moor House from top to bottom until it glittered, arrange the furniture, fill the fires with coal and bake endlessly. St. John was slightly dissatisfied. He thought that she would grow bored with time. St. John would give her two months before she would get bored with her new activity at Moor House before she should find something else to spend her time doing. Jane wanted to be as content as as queen, not enveloped in restlessness again. St. John didn't want her talents going to waste. Jane wanted to be happy and meant to be happy.

Hannah and Jane worked endlessly and joyfully. Jane had bought new furniture, carpets and curtains, ornaments for tables, and so on. When they were finished, Moor House was wonderfully redecorated. When Thursday arrived, Hannah and Jane were dressed and ready for Mary and Diana's arrival. St. John arrived first. Jane had warned him from coming near the house until everything was ready. Jane took him on a tour of the house—he thought that she must have worked very hard to have changed so much in a short space of time, but said nothing to indicate his happiness with it. Jane wondered if she had changed too much—if she had disrespected something related to his memory of the house. St. John assured her she had respected everything and had thought more seriously about the house than he thought she would. He asked where a particular book was, she showed him, and he sat down to read it. Jane did not like this—she began to believe what he said about being hard and cold. The general pleasures of life meant nothing to him—he aspired after what was good and great, but would never rest or approve of those resting around him. Jane understood that he would be a poor husband, and that his wife—if he took one—would be frustrated with him. She could see that he would be suited as a missionary. Hannah suddenly yelled that Diana and Mary were arriving. Jane ran out into the dark to meet the coach. Jane kissed them both as they disembarked, and then led them into the house. As the driver and Hannah brought their boxes in, St. John stepped in to greet them. He gave each a quick kiss, said a few words of welcome and then retreated back into the parlour. The two girls were delighted with the house and expressed their gratitude to Jane and Hannah. Jane was sure that her work had met their wishes exactly. That evening was a joyful one, even if their glee seemed to disturb St. John. He appeared to want a calmer time. A boy knocked at the door and asked St. John to come and see his mother who was dying. The house was four miles off, but St. John wanted to go and see to her. Hannah suggested that he shouldn't go as that road was the worst to travel in the dark, but St. John pulled his cloak on and left the house. He did not return until midnight and looked happier for having helped someone. The entire Christmas week frustrated him and he escaped the house often to visit the sick and poor in his parish.

One morning, Diana asked her brother if his plans were fixed. He told them they were and revealed that he would be leaving England the following year. They asked about Rosamond Oliver. He revealed she was about to be married to Mr. Granby, a well connected heir. Diana thought that was quick — they couldn't have known each other for long. St. John told them they had met at a country ball two months before, and that there were no obstacles to the marriage. When Jane found him alone after this news, she was tempted to ask him if the news upset him, but he seemed he didn't need any sympathy. Jane was also out of practice talking to him. He had not kept his promise to treat her like his third sister and constantly made observations about their differences. She lived under the same roof, but the distance between them was larger than it had been when she was just the village schoolmistress. When she remembered how they had confided in one another, she could scarcely believe his coldness. Jane was a little surprised when he looked up at her and told her that the battle was fought and the victory won. She did not immediately reply, but then wondered if he had lost a lot despite his victories. He did not think so, and now his way was clearer and less conflicted.

When the house, Mary and Diana calmed down a little more, St. John spent more time at Moor House. Mary drew, Diana read, Jane studied German and St. John studied Eastern tongues, information necessary to his future plans. Sometimes he would look up from his studies to look at them all and, if caught, would look immediately back at his work. Jane wondered what it meant. She also wondered why he was satisfied by her weekly visit to Morton school, especially during poor weather. He was able to defend her strength to Diana and Mary. When Jane returned, tired and beaten by the weather, she did not complain for fear of annoying him. One afternoon she had to stay at home because she had a cold. Diana and Mary went to Morton in her place, and she sat reading in the same room as St. John. He asked if she was studying German and told her she should start studying Hindi instead. It was the language he was studying at that moment and it would help him to have someone to study with. He had debated asking his sisters, but had decided on Jane because she kept to a task much longer than they did. She would not have to sacrifice her time for long as he would leave in three months. It was not easy to refuse St. John. She agreed. When Diana and Mary returned they laughed and admitted their brother would not have been able to persuade them into studying Hindi. Jane found him a patient, precise master who expected her to do a great amount of work. She could not talk or laugh when he was nearby as she remembered that he did not approve of this kind of behaviour. She followed his every move and need. She did not like her work and wished he would leave her alone. One evening, while his sisters and Jane stood around St. John wishing them a good night, he kissed Mary and Diana on the cheek and took Jane's hand. Diana told him off for not treating her like his third sister and pushed Jane toward St. John. He bent his head and kissed Jane. He stood back to watch her face. She was sure she had not blushed and may have even turned a little pale. Jane wished she could please him, but to do so she had to ignore her own personality and soul to do so and force herself into activities she did not have a natural interest in. He wanted to train her to a high level that Jane knew she could never reach.

She had not forgotten Mr. Rochester amid her new activities and fortune. His name and presence followed her everywhere. She wanted to know what had happened to him, and every night sat in her bedroom thinking about it. In the course of her letters with Mr. Briggs she had asked about Mr. Rochester, but he did not know anything about him. She then wrote to Mrs. Fairfax asking the same thing, but did not receive a reply. This made her extremely anxious. Jane wrote again, thinking that her letter may have been lost but after six months passed with no reply, Jane's hope disappeared. She was very sad. She could not enjoy the Spring or Summer. Diana thought Jane looked ill and wanted her to go to the seaside with her, but St. John opposed this. He wanted her to work, and thought Jane wanted to work. She needed purpose. Even though she knew it was foolish, she could not deny him.

One day she came to her studies in a depression. She had received a letter from Mr. Briggs and foolishly raised her hopes for news about Mr. Rochester. She only received business news instead. As she looked over Hindi, she began to cry again. St. John called Jane over to study at his side, but she could not read without sobbing aloud. Diana and Mary were not in the room, and St. John only told her to calm down for a moment instead of asking why she was crying. He waited patiently for Jane to calm down but did not say anything. She mumbled an excuse about not being well that morning and then succeeded with her task. St. John put their books away and told her she would take a walk with him. Jane wanted to call Diana and Mary to join them, but he only wanted one companion on the walk. She followed his orders and in ten minutes was walking up a wild lane with St. John.

When they reached a rocky area near a waterfall St. John suggested they should sit down for a moment. Jane sat, but St. John stood, looking around him. He would not forget the countryside when he was in a foreign land. He sat down, then, and they did not speak for half an hour. Eventually, St. John told Jane he was leaving in six weeks and would sail to East India. Jane hoped that God would protect him. St. John knew He would as was doing His work. It was strange to him that his friends and family were not gathering around him to join in with his work. Jane argued that not everyone had his strength and it would be foolish for the weak to try and keep up. St. John was only thinking of those who were worthy of the work and able to do it. Jane thought that there were few people like that. St. John agreed. He added that it was best to show these people what their gifts were and to direct them to their tasks. Jane wondered if they would already know what their tasks were if they were already qualified to do it. Jane trembled, scarcely believing what she was hearing. St. John asked her what her heart said to her. Jane's heart was mute and silent. St. John would answer for it: he wanted her to come with him to India.

The hills around her seemed to spin and Jane thought she heard a cry for help, but she could not help. She begged St. John to show her mercy. St. John wanted her as a missionary's wife — as his wife. He did not love her and only valued her for her mental abilities and work. Jane argued she was not fit for it. St. John had seemed to know she would argue in this way as he folded his arms and focused. He was ready for any opposition and would not rest until the argument was resolved in his favour. He argued that her humility — her humbleness — was a clear sign that she was a good Christian and more than fit for the work they would do. Not even St. John thought he was truly worthy of the work, and he did not even understand a missionary's life yet — he had not lived one yet. Jane did not feel anything when he spoke about that kind of future — she could not accomplish what he wanted her to do. St. John had watched her since they first met and had made her his student for ten months.

When she first arrived, she proved that she could run the village school with focus and calm work. She had a clear, calm mind when she heard she had a fortune, and she showed him sacrifice excited her when she split that fortune into four. When Jane took on his studies purely because he wanted her to, she still showed perseverance and worked hard. Her assistance to him would be invaluable. He waited for a moment for an answer. Jane wanted fifteen minutes to think. He walked a little way up the path and sat down there. Jane knew she could do what he wanted her to do. She could see that she was capable of it now, but she did not want her life to be lived under an Indian sun. When she came to die, he would not care for her—he would only be glad she was going to God. If she left England she would be leaving a land that was empty to her. Mr. Rochester did not live in England anymore, and even if he did it had to mean nothing to her. She had to live without him, not live day to day in hopes of news about him or a reunification. If she had to find something to replace her governess position with, she may as well serve God. She felt she should say yes, but she knew if she did she would give her all. All of her effort and strength to make sure that St. John was satisfied with her work ethic. She would not, however, agree to be his wife. They did not love one another—Jane could not be his wife knowing her husband's spirit did not really consider her. She would go as his sister, but not as his wife. Jane got up and told St. John she would go to India only if she could go as a free woman. They were sister and brother.

St. John disagreed — she was not his real sister. They had to marry one another. He urged her to see sense. Jane considered it but she could not agree with him as they did not love one another. St. John reminded her she agreed to go to India with him. Jane reminded him she had conditions to go with that agreement. St. John knew Jane would not oppose going to India once she had made the decision to go. She was usually consistent with her decisions. However, they could only do their work best if they were united in marriage. If they were truly sister and brother, he would not look for a wife as he would have a connection with someone else there. He wanted a wife to influence throughout life and own until death. Jane told him to find someone else — someone more suited to him. She would be a missionary, but she would not give him herself.

St. John urged her to consider: God would not be satisfied with her half sacrifice. He was enlisting Jane under God's name and she would have to make an entire sacrifice. Jane would give her heart to God, but not to St. John—he would have her body, but not her soul or heart. Jane had feared St. John until this moment because she had not understood him, but now she saw his faults because he showed emotion. He revealed his true nature to her. Jane knew she was standing with no Saint, but with an equal, and knew she could resist and argue with him. St. John argued that he only wanted her to give God her heart, and then she would be ready to do whatever she needed to do to spread Christianity across the globe. She will not need to think about her own personal feelings—she will simply enter into the marriage with him. Jane imagined what it would be like to be his wife. She could not. Her heart and mind might be free, but she would still be physically entrapped. She would suffer for a long time—she would not be able to be herself, and she would not be able to cry out. She again told St. John she would go with him as a missionary, but not as his wife. She would not be a part of him. St. John coldly told her that she had to become part of him or the bargain was off. He could not take a nineteen year old girl with him to India unless they were married. They could not be among tribes if they were not wed. Jane replied that he could if they were truly siblings, or if Jane was a man. St. John argued that everyone knew they were not siblings, and he could not introduce her as one. And she could not be a man—while she had a man's intelligence, she had a woman's heart. Jane argued that her woman's heart was also capable of respect, frankness and submission to her supervisor.

t. John began speaking to himself, demanding that they had to be married and that there was no other way. They would have enough love between them. Jane scorned his idea of love and marriage, and him for offering them. Jane could not tell from his face how he felt. He didn't think he deserved her scorn—he had done nothing. Jane asked him to forgive the way she spoke, but it was his fault for frustrating her. The nature of love was a topic that neither of them should discuss as they would never see eye to eye on it. She begged him to abandon his idea of marriage. St. John could not: it was something he had thought about for a long time, but he would not continue to argue with her about it. He would leave the next day for Cambridge and would return in two weeks for her answer. He reminded her that if she denied him, she was denying God as well. If she refused to be his wife, she would sink into a lazy, selfish, obscure life. He turned away.

As they walked home side by side, Jane knew what his silence meant. He was disappointed in Jane. He had expected her submission and met with resistance instead. It was as a man that he wanted her to obediently follow his every whim, but it was as a Christian that he met her resistance with patience. That night, after St. John kissed his sisters, he forgot to shake Jane's hand and left the room. Jane had thought she had no love for him at all, but found she was hurt by the omission. Diana could see that they had been arguing and sent her into the hall to find him. He would be expecting her. Jane did not have enough pride to stop her from seeking happiness, and went to find him. She told him to shake her hand. He shook it coldly without smiles or happy words. When Jane asked if he had forgiven her, he only replied that he had not been offended and there was nothing to forgive. He left her in the hall, and Jane wished he had knocked her over.

Chapter Thirty-Five:

St. John did not leave for Cambridge the next day as promised. He hung around the house for an entire extra week and made Jane feel unwelcome in the house. The punishment that stern, conscientious people are able to inflict on others without needing to say anything was St. John's chosen path, and Jane knew she was well beyond his favour. Jane knew he would not have harmed a hair on her head even if he had the power to do so, but she knew he had not forgotten her scorn for him and his love. She had been forgiven but those words would hang between them for forever. He continued to call Jane to his desk as usual to study and still spoke to her, but to Jane he was only marble and not flesh and blood. Jane felt tortured. Her grief built up in her slowly. She knew if she became his wife it would kill her without even drawing a single drop of blood. He did not care for Jane's feelings and did not seem to have any of his own. His sisters were kinder than usual, however.

The night before he left for home, Jane happened to see him walking around in the garden. She remembered that he had saved her life once and that they were near relations. She wanted to make friends with him again, so went out into the garden and spoke to him. She told him she was unhappy because he was angry with her and she wanted to be friends again with him. St. John hoped they were friends. Jane told him he didn't see the difference between their past and present, but St. John assured her he didn't mean her any ill will. Jane believed he was incapable of wishing ill will on anyone, but she wanted more affection from him than she would receive if they were strangers. St. John told her, in a cool, calm tone, that they were more than strangers. Jane wanted to step away from him but she wanted his friendship still. It was valuable to her, and she would fight for it. She asked him if he would leave her without a kind word when he went to India. St. John turned to her then — they were going to India together. He would not be leaving her! Jane reminded him that he would let her go unless they were married and she would not marry him. He asked why she refused him. Originally, Jane did not want to marry him because he did not love her and now because he almost hates her. If they married, she would die — he was killing her then and now.

St. John turned very pale—she should not have said what she did as they were evidence of a sinful mind. Jane knew he truly hated her and she would not try to be friends. They were now enemies. St. John reacted with emotion and Jane knew she had caused him pain. She took his hand and assured him she did not mean to upset him. He thought that she meant to come to India with him after all. Jane would go as his assistant. Silence followed. He told her that her common sense should have led her to accept his suggestion. Jane interrupted him and told him to use his common sense. He could not be totally shocked by her decision. He must have expected it. St. John would not accept her as a travelling sister, but she seemed sincere in her offer and he would talk to a married missionary in town. He had a wife who needed an assistant and Jane would do nicely. Jane was not under any obligation to go to India with anyone else, especially with strangers. She was going to India because Jane loved St. John as a sister. If she went—whomever she went with— she would not live for very long in the climate. God did not give her life for her to throw it away, and if she went she would die very soon in. She also had to know if she would be of any use in England before she left it. St. John guessed that she meant Mr. Rochester. Her interest in him was lawless. She admitted she wanted to find out what had happened to him. St. John would remember her in his prayers and hope that she did not get led astray. He had thought she was one of the chosen ones, but he guessed not.

When Jane stepped back into the house, she found Diana standing at the window. Diana looked at her face and commented that Jane was quite pale. She had been watching St. John and Jane talking for half an hour and wondered whether or not he loved her. Jane told her he did not. Diana had thought he did because he was always watching her and forever asking her to sit with him. She and Mary had decided St. John would ask her to marry him. Jane admitted he had already asked. Diana was excited. They had hoped he would. She hoped Jane would marry him so that he would stay in England. Jane told her that he meant her to go to India with him as a labourer. Diana thought the idea was madness and hoped she had not agreed to go with him. Diana was glad she would not be going—Jane would have died under the extreme fatigue. St. John would have pushed her to the extreme and not allowed her to rest. Diana had watched Jane do whatever he wanted her to do and assumed that she loved him. Jane did not love him as she would love a husband, even though he was handsome. Jane thought she was too plain and they wouldn't be well suited. Diana thought she was very pretty and too good to die of fatigue and heat-stroke in India. She begged Jane to give up any consideration she might give the trip to India. Jane assured her she had, especially after he accused her of being indecent when she suggested they go as sister and brother. Diana wondered how Jane knew he did not love her. Jane told her that he explained he only wanted to marry her for labour, not love. He believed Jane was not formed for love. If that was true, then she wasn't formed for marriage either. She admitted that St. John was talented and heroic looking, and she might have fallen in love with him. He would not want her to love him, and if she showed any love for him he would call her indecent. He was a good man, but he has forgotten how normal people felt and feel, and so people should keep out of his way just in case it stopped his progress. Jane saw him coming, then, and left Diana alone.

She was forced to sit with him at supper. He acted as he always had. Jane thought he would not speak to her, but he seemed to have forgiven her once again. That evening he read for them from the Bible. It was usually pleasant to listen to his voice and he often impressed the ladies with his noble, solemn and thrilling tone of voice. He turned toward Jane at one point and stared at her while he read. He read that the fearful and unbelieving would end up in Hell. Jane knew what St. John feared for her. St. John clearly believed he already had a place in Heaven and longed for the day when he would join God. In the prayer that followed the read chapter, he asked for strength and guidance for the weak-hearted stragglers tempted by sin. Jane was amazed by his strength and goodness. When it was over, Diana and Mary kissed St. John and left the room. Jane wished him a good journey for the next day. St. John reminded her that he would return from Cambridge in two weeks and expect her to think about his offer. If he had listened to his pride, he would not have offered his hand in marriage again, but he listened to his duty to God. He laid his hand on Jane's head and spoke to her like a pastor, not a brother. Jane was tempted to stop resisting him and agree to go, but she knew it was wrong to do so. However, Jane forgot her oppositions. She was paralysed. Visions of Angels and God filled her head and religion seemed to call her. St. John gently asked if she would be able to decide then. Jane knew that his nature would not change with time—he might be gentle to get his way, but he would still be hard and cold. Jane would marry him if she knew it was God's will. St. John was glad his prayers had been heard and pulled Jane into his arms almost as if he loved her. Jane knew the difference as she had already been held by someone who truly loved her. She cried out to Heaven to show her the way and she suddenly felt a strange shock go through her entire body. St. John asked her what she saw. Jane only heard her name repeated over and over. It was the voice of Edward Fairfax Rochester who spoke to her in pain and urgently. Jane cried that she was coming for him and ran out into the garden. She asked where he was. The hills only echoed her voice back to her. Jane left St. John and told him not to follow her or ask questions. Jane went back to her room, fell on her knees and prayed. She lay down on her bed eager for daylight.

Chapter Thirty-Six:

When daylight came, Jane rose at dawn and got her things ready for her absence from the house. She heard St. John come out of his room and stop at her door. Jane was afraid he would knock on the door, but he only slipped a piece of paper under it. It reminded her that he wanted a clear decision when he returned in two weeks, and that she should pray not to fall into temptation. Jane's mental reply to him defended her own spirit, which knew what was right and wrong and she would find her own path. Jane watched St. John leave the house and walk across the moors toward Whitecross. Jane would take the same path soon to meet her own coach. It was still too early for breakfast, so Jane paced in her room thinking about the voice she had heard and the sensation she felt the previous night. It seemed as if the voice had come from inside her and she wondered if it had appeared due to nerves or sudden inspiration. She would finally know what happened to Mr. Rochester.

At breakfast, Jane announced she was going on a journey for at least four days and would be going alone to see or discover news about an old friend. Diana wondered if Jane was well enough to travel as she looked very pale. Jane was only anxious and the journey would hopefully ease her nerves. While the sisters could have pried into her plans, they asked no other questions and let her prepare for her journey. She left Moor House at 3pm and waited for the coach at Whitecross which would take her to Thornfield. When it approached, Jane saw it was the same coach that had brought her here a year before. She would not have to give up all of her possessions to travel it this time, however. As the coach sped towards Thornfield, Jane felt like she was going home.

Two days later, Jane recognized the moors of Morton and asked the coach driver how far they were from Thornfield Hall. It was only two miles, so she got out of the coach, gave her box of things to someone for keeping and started to walk. The nearby inn was called "The Rochester Arms" and Jane was giddy to know she was almost there. She knew she should go inside the inn to ask if Mr. Rochester was actually in the area or had left for Europe, but she could not, fearing a reply that would send her spiralling into despair. Prolonging her hope meant prolonging her despair. She ran by the stile and the woods, and then came nearer to the house. She wondered if Mr. Rochester would be standing in the window and told herself not to run toward him if he was. She slipped into the orchard and peeped out from behind a pillar to see if any bedroom blinds were up. When she took a peep, she stepped out in front of the house. The house was in ruins! The grounds were wasted and the front of the house had no roof, battlements or chimney. There were no glass panes in the windows, either. The house was deathly silent.

Jane knew now why her letters had gone unanswered: there was no one here to answer them. She wondered what had happened, but there was no one around to tell her. After Jane wondered around the ruins, she realized that the house had been in ruins for months. Snow and rain had beaten the ground among the debris because grass and weeds grew between stones and rafters. Jane wondered where Mr. Rochester was, but she would not find her answers there. She would only find her answers at the inn. She returned and asked the owner to bring her some breakfast and talk quietly with her for a while. Jane managed to overcome her shock to ask him about Thornfield Hall. He had lived there once serving the late Mr. Rochester. Jane asked if Mr. Rochester was dead! The innkeeper explained he had served Mr. Rochester's father. Jane could breathe again knowing her own Mr. Rochester was still alive. He explained that Thornfield Hall burned down around harvest-time in Autumn in the dead of night. The building was completely on fire before anyone arrived to help. Jane asked if they discovered why it caught fire. He mentioned the lunatic in the house who was kept in confinement and retold the tale about the discovery that she was his wife.

Jane tried to put him back on subject, but he insisted on telling her about a young woman Mr. Rochester fell in love with. Jane stopped him halfway through the tale and asked if the lunatic had set the fire. She had. Mrs. Poole always kept a bottle of gin with her and drank too much that night. Mrs. Rochester took the keys out of her pocket, set fire to the room next door, and then went down to the governess' room. The innkeeper added at this point that the governess had been missing for two months and Mr. Rochester had searched for her endlessly. He had sent Mrs. Fairfax away from him and gave her a salary for life, and Miss Adele was sent to school. He saw no one and shut himself up in the house. He did not leave England for Europe. Mr. Rochester had been at home when the fire started and he made sure the servants got out of the house before going up to his lunatic wife's room to help her. She was on the roof waving her arms and screaming. Mr. Rochester stepped onto the roof behind her and called his wife to her, but she yelled and jumped to her death. Jane asked about Mr. Rochester. He was alive, but the innkeeper thought he would be better off dead. Jane pushed him to explain himself. Mr. Rochester was blind. After Mrs. Rochester had jumped from the roof, the battlements had caved in. He had been hurt, his eyesight irreparably damaged and a hand had to be amputated. He was a blind cripple living in a manor house at Ferndean. Only two people stayed with him as servants as he would have no one else with him. Jane asked if the innkeeper had a coach or carriage. They did. Jane asked it to be readied so she could go to Ferndean immediately.

Chapter Thirty-Seven:

The manor house at Ferndean was an old building of medium size. Jane had heard of it from Mr. Rochester before as he often went there. His father had purchased it and would have rented it out had it not been in the middle of nowhere. It remained empty and unfurnished with the exception of two or three rooms for when he went shooting. Jane arrived there on a dark evening, walking the rest of the last mile on foot. The woods and foliage surrounding the house showed no way in and Jane wondered for a moment if she had taken a wrong turn until they opened up to reveal the house. It was a lonely house. A door opened slowly and a figure stepped out with his hand outstretched to see if it was raining. Jane recognized him: it was Mr. Rochester! Jane kept quiet and still for a moment to watch him. He was still an athletic looking man but looked desperate and sad. Jane wanted to go to him and kiss him on the forehead and lips, but she wouldn't yet. Mr. Rochester stepped down and stopped, unsure which way to go. He lifted a hand, opened his glazed eyes and stared toward the sky. He stretched his right hand out, for his left arm was strapped to his chest, to see what was around him but only met with air. He folded his arms and stood quietly with the rain pouring on his head. His servant, John, appeared and asked if Mr. Rochester wouldn't take his arm and go inside. Mr. Rochester wanted to be left alone. John left without noticing Jane. Mr. Rochester tried to walk around but he was uncertain where everything was and went back to the door.

Jane went to the door herself and knocked on it. John's wife, Mary, opened it and Jane wished her well. Mary looked like she had seen a ghost. Jane was led inside to the kitchen where she explained everything that had happened to her since she had left Thornfield and that she had come to see Mr. Rochester. She wondered if she could stay at the house for the night. She could. At that moment, a bell rang from the parlour. Jane asked Mary to tell Mr. Rochester he had a visitor but not to give him her name. Mary warned her that he saw no one. She returned a moment later and told Jane she had to send in her name and business. Mary put together a tray of water and glasses. Jane asked to take the tray in herself. It shook as Jane held it and stepped into the parlour.

The parlour itself was gloomy and dark. Mr. Rochester leaned on the mantelpiece. His old dog, Pilot, lay on the floor and bounded towards her when he saw Jane. Jane set the tray on a table. Mr. Rochester told the dog to lie down and turned to see what the commotion was all about, but obviously could not see anything. He asked for the water to be handed to him. She approached with Pilot following behind her, still excited. Mr. Rochester asked Jane if she was Mary. Jane told him that Mary was in the kitchen. He stretched out with his hand but did not manage to touch her. He asked who she was, and then demanded she reveal herself to him. Jane admitted she had arrived that day and that John and Mary knew she was with him. Mr. Rochester thought he was going mad. If he could not touch her, he thought he might die. Jane gave him her hand and he was astounded that it was "her" small fingers. He reached up her arm, her shoulder, neck and waist. He asked if it was Jane — this was her body. Jane admitted it was her — she was there in voice and heart, too. She was glad to be near him again. He could not believe she was really there, but she pointed out he could hold her, so she must be there. He thought he was dreaming her up, but it was not a dream. She promised she would never leave him again.

Mr. Rochester thought she was just a vision and he would wake up, as usual, to find her words empty. He had been abandoned, lonely and hopeless, and his dreams always fled. This one would too. Before she went, though, he wanted to embrace her. Jane pressed her lips to his eyelids, kissed his brow and suddenly he seemed to believe she was really there and come back to him. He could scarcely believe it. He thought she was dead in a ditch or living as an outcast among strangers. Jane told him she was independent. She had five thousand pounds to her name. Mr. Rochester knew he would not dream about practical matters like fortunes. Jane told him if she wouldn't let her live with him, she would build a house near to his and he could sit in her parlour when he wanted company in the evening. Mr. Rochester didn't understand: if she was rich, then she would have friends and would not be lonely. Jane was her own mistress and she would stay with him if she was allowed. She would be his neighbour, nurse, housekeeper, companion. He would not be lonely anymore while she still lived. He could not reply. He opened his mouth to say something and then shut it again. Jane felt a little bit ashamed and wondered if he, like St. John, thought her behaviour was inappropriate.

Jane had made her proposal with a hint that she might be his wife, but he hadn't responded at all. Jane began to gently move out of his arms, but he pulled her closer. He told her she could not go. His soul wanted her. Jane told him she would stay — she has already said so. Mr. Rochester thought they were not talking about the same kind of staying. He teased her that she could only think of him as a fatherly figure now that he needed help to get around and do things. Jane would be content to be his nurse if he thought it was for the best, but Mr. Rochester wanted her to marry. Jane did not care about being married. He fell into another gloomy mood, but Jane knew that she had not been mistaken and felt her shame slip away. She told him someone had to make him human again as he had long hair like a lion. She wondered if he had grown his nails like bird claws, or not. He showed her his mutilated arm — he had no hand or nails on this arm. He asked her if he thought it a horrid sight. She was sorry to see it and his eyes, and the scar on his forehead, but she loved him too much. Mr. Rochester thought she would be horrified when she saw his wounds. Jane told him not to think about it. She had to leave him for a moment to build a fire and sweep the hearth. She asked if he could tell when there was a good fire lit. He could see a glow through his right eye, and he could see a cloud where the candles were, but he could not see Jane but was happy to hear and touch her. He did not take supper anymore, but Jane was hungry and she was sure he only forgot.

Jane called Mary into the room and they had it in cheerful order very quickly. Jane prepared him a supper. Jane was at complete ease around him because she knew what suited him. It brought her to life again. He smiled, showed clear joy and had warmth in his face. He asked her many questions after supper about her past, but she only gave him small replies. She did not want to talk everything over that night as it was late, and she only wanted to cheer him up. He was not overly happy, though, and occasionally had to check that Jane was a real human being. He thought she was an enchantment. His life had been a dark and hopeless one for months. He had done nothing, expected nothing and felt nothing but cold and sadness and a desire to be near Jane again. He was sure that she would be gone the next day. Jane decided to provide him with a practical reply and promised to apply something to his scorched eyebrows to make them grow back. He didn't see the point of that if she would disappear again. She asked him if he had a comb on him. She wanted to comb his hair out. He asked her if he was hideous. She told him he always had been. He told her she had not lost her wickedness. Jane had been with good people — better than him and more refined. Mr. Rochester wondered who she had been with. Jane told him he had to wait until the next day to hear her tale from beginning to end. Mr. Rochester told her he had not felt this way for a year. Now that his hair was combed, Jane told him she'd go to bed. Mr. Rochester asked her if she was only staying with ladies to which she laughed and ran upstairs. She was pleased she could bring him out of his sadness by teasing him.

The next morning, Jane heard Mr. Rochester get up and wander from one room to another. When Mary got up he asked her which room he put her into and if she would go and ask Jane to come down for breakfast. Jane came down for breakfast as soon as she thought there would be food to eat. Jane had a chance to look at him before he discovered she was there. He sat in his chair but was not the Mr. Rochester of the past. She wanted to be happy and carefree, but his powerless made her freeze for a moment. She told him that they should go for a walk in the sun and his face lit up to hear she was still in the house and had not vanished. He had been listening to the birds but nothing was as pleasing as Jane's voice — her presence was like sunshine to him. Jane's eyes watered, but she brushed the tears away and prepared breakfast.

They spent most of the morning in the open air walking around the countryside. They found a quiet little spot to sit on and Mr. Rochester pulled Jane onto his lap. Pilot lay near them. Mr. Rochester was upset that she had abandoned him at Thornfield and he failed to find her. When he discovered that she had not taken any money or jewellery with her, he thought of her as poor and outcast somewhere. He asked her to tell her story. Jane told him about the events of the previous year and made sure to skip over some of her three days of starvation because she did not want to inflict more pain on him. What he did hear upset him: he wished she had confided in him and asked for help. Jane assured him her suffering had been short lived and then told him about Moor House. Mr. Rochester asked about St. John when his name was mentioned and wondered if Jane liked him. Jane admitted that he was a good man, twenty-nine years old and aimed to perform great things in his life. His brain was active, but he did not talk much, had good manners and was a handsome man. Jane admitted she liked him, pretending not to see what Mr. Rochester was really getting at. He was jealous of St. John.

Mr. Rochester asked if she would not want to sit on his lap anymore. Jane didn't know why she would get up. He suggested that she had found a handsome man. Mr. Rochester interrogated her about him and his treatment of Jane. Eventually, Mr. Rochester reached the subject of marriage and Jane admitted he had asked her to marry him. Mr. Rochester told her she could leave his knee but she was comfortable there. Mr. Rochester didn't know how she could be comfortable when she was clearly in love with St. John. Jane told him to push her off because she wouldn't get up by herself. Jane could not go to St. John because he was not her husband and would never be. They did not love one another. He only wanted to marry to make her his missionary's wife, and she was never happy by his side. Why would she leave Mr. Rochester for him? Mr. Rochester asked her to confirm this was true. Jane did: she had only wanted to make him a little jealous and less sad. She thought anger was better than grief. She loved Mr. Rochester so much and she wanted to stay with him for forever.

Mr. Rochester kissed her and damned his blindness and lost hand. He cried and compared himself to the split chestnut tree in the Thornfield orchard. Jane disagreed and pointed out that plants, his friends, would grow in his roots and lean towards him for protection. Mr. Rochester told her he didn't want a friend—he wanted a wife. He wanted *her* for his wife and asked her to marry him. She agreed to marry him again and again—after e provided her with every excuse she might have for refusing him. Jane thought that she was being rewarded for something she did well in life. She would be as happy as anything to be his wife. Mr. Rochester thought it was because she loved sacrifice, but Jane did not know what she was sacrificing—she was with the man she loved and could be useful to him. Mr. Rochester wanted to marry her immediately, and Jane could see the old impulsiveness rising in him. She told him that it was late in the afternoon and that they should return home. He agreed and wanted the third day from then to be their wedding day. He did not care about jewels and other finery; he just wanted to marry her.

Mr. Rochester rambled out loud. He was grateful to God. He had done wrong and had suffered, but he had experienced remorse and regret lately and began to pray. Late last Monday night he had been in a deep grief and told God, if He agreed, that he should take Mr. Rochester's life. He sat by the open window and longed for Jane. He asked God if he had suffered enough, and if he could have peace and happiness once more. He pleaded with God and then spoke Jane's name out loud in a frenzy. After this, he had heard Jane's voice telling him she was coming to him. The sound appeared to have come from the mountains or hills, and not from the dull thick woods around Ferndean. It was almost as if he was meeting Jane in that moment.

It had been a Monday night when Jane had received her strange summons—hearing her name aloud, and it had been the exact words Mr. Rochester heard that she had spoken in reply. She did not tell him—she did not want Mr. Rochester to think about the supernatural. Mr. Rochester was sure she could understand why he had doubted she was really there the previous night. He thought she was another vision. He thanked God she was not. He slipped Jane off his knee, took his hat off his head and looked at the ground in silent thought and prayer. He stretched out his hand to Jane to be led. She took hold of his dear hand, kissed it, and than placed it around her shoulder. They entered the wood and headed home.

Chapter Thirty-Eight:

The wedding was a quiet affair. Only Mr. Rochester, Jane, the Clerk and the Parson were present. When they arrived home from the Church, Mary and John were busy in the kitchen. Jane announced that they had been married that morning. Mary startled. She held a ladle in the air for a full three minutes before she reacted. She asked Jane if she was sure. John grinned. He had told his wife how things would end up. He wished them both joy. Jane told them Mr. Rochester wanted them to have a gift, and then handed them both a five pound note. She left the kitchen. Some time later, she passed outside the door and heard them talking. They thought Jane would do Mr. Rochester a great deal of good—more than any other woman would have done.

Jane wrote to Moor House and Cambridge immediately to tell them her news and explained why she acted the way she did. Diana and Mary approved. Diana would give her some time, and then would come and visit them. Jane did not know how St. John took the news because he did not answer the reply. After six months, she did receive a letter from him which did not mention Mr. Rochester's name or her marriage to him. He continued to maintain a regular correspondence with her and hoped she was happy. Jane went to see Adele at the school she had been placed in as soon as she could. Adele was pale and thin, and was very unhappy. The rules of the school were far too strict for a child of her age and Jane took her home with her. She expected to be a governess again, but found Mr. Rochester needed her help far more. She found a better school for Adele and visited her often. Jane made sure Adele never needed anything and she grew up with a strong English eduction and became a good tempered, docile woman.

Jane had been married for ten years. She knew what it was to live with and for what she loved best on the earth and knew she had been blessed. Jane did not think any woman could be any closer to her husband than Jane was to Mr. Rochester. They did not tire of one another's company and they were always together. Mr. Rochester continued to be blind for the first two years of their marriage and Jane thought this might have brought them closer together as Jane had to be his eyes and right hand. Jane did not grow tired of describing the countryside around them or reading to him. One morning, while Jane wrote a letter Mr. Rochester was dictating, he asked Jane if she was wearing something around her neck and was wearing her pale blue dress. She was. Mr. Rochester had thought that the clouding in his right eye was clearing up, and now he was certain it was. They went to London to see a specialist and Mr. Rochester eventually regained his sight in that eye. He could not read or write much, but he could see without being led by the hand and the world was no longer dark to him. When Jane placed their first born into his arms and saw his boy had inherited his old eyes, Mr. Rochester observed that God had been merciful.

Diana and Mary both married and they exchanged visits with Jane every year. Diana's husband was a captain in the navy and Mary's was a clergyman. St. John left for India and continued to pursue his missionary work with focus and energy. He was still unmarried and would never marry—Jane had received a letter from him recently that made her cry. He was dying and would soon join God in Heaven. Jane did not know why she would cry for him when he did not fear death but would embrace it.

84224241R00110

Made in the USA
Middletown, DE
18 August 2018